Wise Food Mind

An Eight Step FOODLOVE Program for LDS Families

Changing Your Relationship with Food
for Optimal Spiritual, Emotional and Physical Health

By Heather B Schauers

Dedicated to my beloved parents, who taught me to value wisdom; and to my husband and children who loved me as I learned how to be wise.

Contents

Introduction

"Wisdom is nothing more than healed pain."

Robert Gary Lee, Playwright

Where I'm Coming From

Mormon prophesied that the Lord would remember the covenant which he made with Israel in a day when "there shall be great pollutions upon the face of the earth."[1] To get right to the theme of this book—the food we eat and the way we eat it has become polluted, or corrupt, and these factors combined with the stress of modern life can be toxic.

Unfortunately, having full use of our divine potential is nearly impossible when we are bogged down by mental and physical illness; chronic pain and strong negative emotions are fertile ground for Satan to use his tools to undermine our efforts for good, turn us inward, and take our agency. An effective tool of the adversary in the last days is an unhealthy relationship with corrupt food.

I'm writing this because my unhealthy relationship with food was robbing my health, and changing that relationship helped me reclaim health. Not only that, but my experience brought me closer to Heavenly Father and gave me greater access to my spiritual senses, which enhanced my ability to fight the adversary and be the person I wanted to be. Through truth and light I was not only helped, I was healed and transformed.

I have belabored over my words to make sure I am sharing correct information, and doing so required prayer and willingness to listen to the spirit of truth. My reader must also be willing to listen to this spirit, and I invite you to scrutinize my words and find the truth that I hope to provide.

---

[1] The Book of Mormon, Mormon 8:31

This is not a diet program. I'm not on a "strict diet;" in fact, there is a lot of talk about how dieting only makes relationships with food more toxic.[2] Through research and inspiration I've come up with an optimal eating lifestyle (I adhere to this way of eating for life), and with that I've developed a love and appreciation for food and the life food gives us. This book is about that knowledge and the sacrifices that gave my life back, and how you can do the same. My story is shared in detail in the second part of this introduction, explaining why and how I came up with a way to change eating habits and reclaim health.

Where You Come From

What ails you? Are you tired every day? Do you have unexplainable dizzy spells or pain? Headaches? Indigestion? Or maybe you feel a lack of motivation, indifference about life, or feel downright depressed? Do you take medications you wish you didn't, or find little help from your doctors? Here is an account from a LDS mother with similar issues:

> I'm so discouraged and overwhelmed. Ever since I had my baby my weight is making me so depressed. I know it's from years of abusing my body with sugar and the wrong kind of carbs. I've been researching lately about food and it just leaves me upset, it seems like everything I eat is bad for me. I look through healthy cookbooks and I don't know a lot of ingredients and haven't a clue to buy the proper equipment. With having a baby I have so little energy these days, and always end up making something fast and convenient, which is why I can't lose weight. I feel like all my efforts to lose weight will never work. Even when I trained for the half marathon and was eating the best I ever had, I didn't lose it. It is one of my biggest fears to become obese, and to not have enough strength to raise a family.

---

[2] Mary O'Malley *The Gift of Our Compulsions*

I just don't know what to do. We don't have much money right now, and bad food is cheap. I have no idea how to cook fancy things or where to buy the right kind of food. I so want to be healthy, I want to love my body, and I want my kids to be healthy. But I am so weak I seem to always cave into my cravings or to keep on buying the easy-to-make food.[3]
If any of this sounds familiar you are in the right place. The problems of how to change eating habits, heal the body, recover energy, and feel good emotionally are difficult in our culture. Additionally, it is extremely overwhelming to think about changing something that keeps us going in a world of stress.

Many people tell me "I could never do that" and I understand why. It is hard! We are trained from infancy to use food as a coping tool to help us feel better, and there are *many* foods today that are designed to be desirable and make people feel good! It was terrifying for me when I decided to let go of comfort foods and positively confront eating habits I knew were bringing me pain. I needed support from someone who had been there who could carry me through the process, and that is what I want this book to be for anyone else attempting this journey.

This book is designed for members of the LDS church who have unexplained health challenges, mood problems, fatigue or are suffering spiritually and suspect their diet might have something to do with it. I do not address serious food-associated disorders, life threatening allergies, or body dysmorphic disorders. If you suspect you may have one of these issues, please see a mental health professional or your physician.

There is a Better Way

Many of you may already be convinced that how you eat is not the best, and that it may be causing you unnecessary pain and

---

[3] Quote used with permission, wishes to remain anonymous

suffering. Others may be confused about the relationship between food and illness, or don't have enough of a problem to care if there is a relationship. Some may even rather take the consequences and eat what they want because trying to do anything about it seems overwhelmingly stressful (which has negative digestive consequences as well). These are normal and common feelings. In this world where many people are confused and contradicting answers are given, with no basis or standard to live by, what and how to eat can become charged with as many emotions as a political debate!

My hope is to convert you to the idea that there is an answer and, though not as black and white as the Ten Commandments, that answer is more simple than you may have thought. The truth God shared with me? Eating whole foods the way God created them, and limiting sweets, is how you will gain the most benefit from your food. Simple, but not easy if you are eating a convenient, processed, standard American diet. I changed and you can too! I wish to help you apply a healthy view of food principles while getting back to basics which may help alleviate the difficulty of the change process.

One caution to keep in mind from the start: it is not true that any food is "bad," but some foods cause us to "feel bad." You are not "bad" for wanting food that is unhealthy; in fact, you are programmed to be hungry and eat food that is enjoyable and enticing. However, "there is a consequence to how you direct your energies."[4] What and how we eat affects not only how we feel physically, but also emotionally, mentally and spiritually, and may cause long term consequences. I hope to direct your energies toward guarding your eating lifestyle.

We are a Zion people. We are set apart from the world, a light and the salt of the earth.[5] We need full access to our physical and

---

[4] Gudni Gunnarsson, quoted in lecture at "Future of Healing" conference psychologyofeating.com
[5] *The New Testament* Matthew 5:13-14

mental and spiritual capabilities so that we can usher in the great and millennial day! If you choose to read on, and participate in this eight step FOODLOVE program, you and your children will effectively face and solve the problems created by food insults in the last days. This will allow you to have full capacity of your brain function, better control of your moods, more motivation to work and live, and the ability to consistently handle food cravings, make wise food choices for better health now, and prevent health problems in the future.

Additionally, you will have greater power over the adversary whose goal is to limit our agency and keep us miserable. I further assert that by going through this process, you will not only feel better, you will have a life transformation by having more peace, more patience, more gratitude, and more wisdom. After all, Zion is comprised of the "pure in heart."[6]

The Program

Each chapter is designed to take about ten days. This gives you time to read the information and do outside reading and exercises that will prepare you for the next step. You can go at your own pace, however, it would be wise to not take this too quickly. The body and brain need time to adjust to new information and habits in order for the change to be effective.

FOODLOVE is an acronym for each ten day step of the program.

- Food Corruptions and Awareness
- Observe Inside Forces
- Observe Outside Forces
- Dare to Change
- Loving Food and Life
- Optimal Diet Lifestyle
- Vitality, a Choice
- Educating Children

---

[6] D&C 97:21

I hope this will be an answer to prayer for many people confused about what may be causing their spiritual, mental, and physical difficulties. I hope to convince my reader that you have power to change, and to convert you to continue the higher way of eating wisely.

"Go ye out from Babylon. Be ye clean that bear the vessels of the Lord."[7]

My Story

I was born in Provo, Utah in 1978, the first of ten children, and sixth generation of pioneer ancestors on both sides. My parents were members of the Church of Jesus Christ of Latter-Day Saints, as were their parents, and their parents before them. I, too, am a member of this church and feel blessed to be so.

I learned many good things from my parents. We had a garden in my youth and enjoyed lots of fresh-grown vegetables. My dad made his own wheat bread, which I loved, and on Sundays we had a nice home cooked meal of something like roast, potatoes, and vegetables. However, my parents' nutrition education was based on the assumptions of the time, so there were few restrictions on sugar, junk food, or processed food intake. Processed foods, like cereal, were a staple. At the time, all baby boomers were feeding their kids the same way: a mix of the old ways and the new ways, grateful for the convenience and time saved by the new ways.

My parents noticed at a young age that I would get very moody and impatient if I hadn't eaten in a while. They labeled me as "hypoglycemic" and tried their best to keep me fed. I learned quickly how to make myself convenience foods because in my sheltered life there was nothing more torturous than being hungry.

---

[7] Doctrine & Covenants 133:5, The Book of Mormon 3rd Nephi 20:41, Old Testament Isaiah 52:11

I had a fast metabolism and never weighed more than one hundred pounds. At around age eighteen, I started exercising more regularly and I was in pretty good shape. My whole life I'd kept the Word of Wisdom, so I gave the credit for being thin to that. Besides, I'd watched all the videos in health class about anorexia and bulimia. I didn't care how fat I got, I was going to eat and love my food. I thought diets were just for people who were self-conscious and overly concerned about their looks.

I remember the first time I had a notion that what I was eating affected my health. I was sitting in a college class in the fall of 1998 when a sudden sharp pain in my abdomen drove me to the restroom where I fainted in the stall. I felt like a huge stone was in my gut, not allowing anything to pass through.

It came to my mind that the white bread I had been eating may have something to do with it, and for a week or so I swore off any refined flour. That helped me get rid of the pain. But not eating rolls and toast was horrible, especially with my grandma's homemade white bread and jam to enjoy. So when I felt better I went back to my regular diet of refined flour. I healed fast when I was young.

When I got married, my emotional instability started to rear its ugly head. A trial of birth control pills that almost made me suicidal, a miscarriage, and then a pregnancy the first couple years of our marriage all wreaked havoc on my adrenals. The sleep deprivation our first baby caused me was like a special form of torture. I thought I would be scarred for life because of it and didn't know how any mother survived it! Staying faithful to my religion gave me strength to live another day. Again, I healed quickly, and soon after weaning my first child I felt normal and ready to try and have another baby.

After my second baby, reading my scriptures was not helping me cope with life anymore. We had moved to Mississippi and my husband was working a lot of hours, so I was alone with a toddler and an infant in a strange place. My biology could not compete with the strain and it was then that postpartum depression set in. I started to think maybe I was not a good person.

After our third child, we moved back to Utah into a family member's basement with my three little children. Life was very bleak for me at that time. Sleep deprivation, transitions, my husband trying to build his own company, (and, unknown to me at the time, poor diet), in combination with my overly-analytical and ever-negative thoughts, all created a perfect storm of personal bitterness and despair. I kept thinking I could pray my way out of it but it never seemed to go away. My marital discord was intense, my mood regulation was horrible, and my self-worth at its lowest. In diagnostic terms, I had Major Depressive Disorder, Severe Episode.

I remember going to the computer and clicking on links that said, "Suicidal? Click here for help." I never attempted to take my life but I didn't want to live. I wished for death, and the only thing that kept me alive was taking care of my children. As much as I didn't want to be there, I did want them to have a mother more, so I kept going. I started counseling and medication, and read a bunch of books on depression, recovery, and the brain. That helped. I started feeling hope that there was a mission for me to accomplish that didn't involve having ten children, for which I felt so ill equipped both physically and mentally.

I went to the temple to discuss life options with the Lord. I didn't want to be selfish, but I also didn't want to have more children and risk another depressive episode (thinking having babies was the reason I got depressed). The Spirit told me there was still "Lillian." That was clear enough. I got off medication, put my trust in the Lord, and we tried for another baby.

Nine months later we were blessed with a daughter whom we named Lillian. She had a heart defect and had Down's Syndrome, and my "mission" quickly shifted to being a mother of a child with special needs. My spiritual tank was full at that time, so I was happy to have Lillian and her special spirit in our home. My doctor had advised me to take antidepressant medication to offset postpartum depression, and for a while that seemed to help.

Lillian was growing and nursing, so the cardiologist suggested we go ahead with her open-heart surgery to have her two missing valves created, even though she was only four months old. Lillian never came home. She spent the last three months of her life in the PICU. I had to share her care with the nurses that watched her around the clock. After three heart surgeries, an artificial valve, opening her chest to offset swelling, gallons of blood transfusions, and many prayers, fasts, and blessings on her behalf, her kidneys and liver started to fail and we had to take her off life support. She returned to her Heavenly Father after seven months and seven days of life on Earth.

I managed my grief and loss by pouring my efforts into getting a master's degree in Social Work. I noticed something had happened to me that year that I had never experienced before: I had gained a lot of weight and it wasn't coming off. I was sure it was just due to the stress of the year and being on and off medication, and figured when I was fully recovered I would lose weight. After all, I was then off medication, exercising and working hard every day. With the Lord's help, I was accepted to the MSW program and started in the summer of 2009.

The first semester I enrolled in an elective course on substance abuse. As part of the class, we were required to abstain from something for three months to appreciate what it is like for recovering addicts to give up their addictions. I chose to abstain from sugar, as it was the only thing I could think of that I would really miss.

I didn't prepare. I thought I would find things to eat as the meals presented themselves. I couldn't find a single thing to eat in my fridge that first morning that didn't have sugar listed as an ingredient. Not *one*. I panicked. I went to the pantry. *Oh good, tuna fish only has tuna and water in it so I can eat it. But what about lunch?* I couldn't eat tuna for every meal! Sugar was in everything: bread, milk, sauces, soups, pasta, packaged meat, canned things, crackers, dressings, juice, cereal, and granola. I cried. I couldn't go off sugar for three months like this. I decided to change my goal: I would not ingest anything with more than three grams of sugar per serving size, and I would not worry about whether it was in my dinner.

I abstained from all desserts and candy for three months. This was a huge success and an absolute failure at the same time, because I hadn't been able to go 100% off sugar for even one day. How naive of me to think I could just stop eating sugar at the drop of an idea. I had sugar for breakfast, lunch, in between meals, dinner, and dessert! I learned a lot about how addicted I was—how much sugar I'd been processing, when cravings hit, what triggered me—and noticed that while limiting my sugar intake, I had more emotional stability and fewer feelings of being weighed down. Interestingly, I lost ten pounds that semester just by abstaining from candy and dessert, even though my stress environment heightened with school and I exercised sporadically.

I went back to my regular sugar habits after that semester but noticed my body didn't feel well when I ate sugar, worse than it usually did. Eating sweets started losing its appeal as I dealt with an upset stomach for an hour afterwards. The stress of school continued to increase and I started getting headaches and colds that made it difficult to function. I went on a month-long, no-dessert/candy contract with my kids in April 2010, hoping that if I laid off the sweets it would help me get through the last month of school. I felt great on graduation day!

A month later, I got up from saying family prayer and the earth opened up and tried to swallow me; I had the worst dizzy spell I'd ever experienced. Feeling it had to do with the quarter of an ice cream pie I'd eaten the day before, I tried to back off sugar again. However, all I could do was manage to eat less at one time. I couldn't stop altogether. Subsequently, I experienced dizzy spells constantly, my heart raced occasionally, and I felt tired all the time. I wanted to sleep all day and night, couldn't recall things I'd learned, and had fog in my brain. My head started to hurt right in the center of my skull, which seemed to spread every day instead of going away. As you can imagine, I thought something was seriously wrong—maybe I was dying.

I went to my physician who ordered a heart stress test and blood lab work. I was concerned about diabetes because of my family history, but my insulin levels and blood sugar levels all looked normal. He referred me to a cardiologist, who said my heart looked perfect from every angle. I went back to my doctor for a follow up because my symptoms worsened instead of getting better. He checked my thyroid and vitamin levels and everything looked normal. So he prescribed me Zoloft, saying that considering my past history, my problem was probably anxiety.

I'd gotten through graduate school without psychotropic medication, I certainly didn't intend to start taking some now. I knew in my heart this was a problem with biology. My moods weren't perfectly regulated, but I was not depressed; in fact, I was more hopeful, grateful, and happy than I had been in years. I'd accomplished a life goal by completing a master's degree, and I had just been offered my dream job as a part time therapist for an LCSW in private practice. Additionally, my husband and I had moved into a beautiful home, we were financially stable, and our marital relationship good. 2011 was my year! But these health problems were undermining my ability to enjoy the life I had worked so hard to create.

I read a book called *The pH Miracle*[8] because an acquaintance had similar health problems and this book helped her to heal. Skeptical that changing diet could have anything to do with dizzy spells, headaches, and chronic fatigue, yet desperate for help, I read the book. It gave me hope, and I decided to try and implement more raw foods into my diet.

---

[8] *The pH Miracle* written by Robert and Shelly Young

I started eating grapefruit and celery for breakfast instead of cereal, and noticed that same day my headache lessened. I chopped, sliced, blended, and pureed every vegetable you can think of, and ate some white meats and fish, for ten days straight. The weirdest thing happened: I lost fifteen pounds and the headaches were gone. I still had some dizzy spells and fatigue, but I had enough proof that what I ate affected how I felt, so I continued this diet for a while.

After about two months, my symptoms changed to weak, constipated, and hungry all the time. I suspected that I was losing weight in a starvation way, not in a good way. My brother suggested maybe I was hypoglycemic, and warned me of the dangers of being chronically low on blood sugar. I read a book on hypoglycemia written twenty years ago[9] and it seemed to describe me. So I tried that diet instead: eating foods every two or three hours that were low on the glycemic index like nuts, meats, veggies, whole fruits, yogurt/cheese, and whole grains like granola.

I started to get my strength back and I gained a little weight. I splurged on desserts now and then, but thought I was doing moderately well. In February 2012 my depression came back. I knew for whatever reason, sugar was the culprit, and I had to be done with candy and desserts for good. I signed a "no candy/desserts contract" for life. I continued eating hypoglycemic style, and, in addition to the ban on obvious sugars, experienced renewed health. Even the bothersome dizzy spells went away for a while.

In 2013 I started slipping in my resolve to eat whole grains. I didn't eat candy or dessert, but I wanted white bread and pasta. (Pizza was a favorite.) I noticed a few health problems that didn't make sense for my age. If I tried to fast, or was sleep deprived, I had headaches, became mean, angry, sad, and longed for death.

I went back to my doctor and told him I never took the Zoloft because I believed my problems were due to some kind of biological

---

[9] Paavo Airola. *Hypoglycemia: A better approach*

12

imbalance. I brought a typed document outlining my symptoms. He took more labs and said everything still looked normal, and he didn't know what to tell me. I just wasn't "sick enough."

So I kept trying to eat well and not worry about it, but thoughts that I might have problems like a fatty acid metabolic disorder or liver disease kept me paranoid. I prayed for direction, and I was able to reach an endocrinologist who specialized in cholesterol. He kindly listened to my case over the phone and said I was functional enough. I was a mother, holding a job, and managing my emotions so he didn't think anything was majorly wrong with me. I took it as an answer to prayer and did not seek any medical intervention all the rest of that year.

In January 2014 I started lifting weights, confident that I was stable enough in my health that I could do things that normal people do to strengthen their bodies. That same month, I deteriorated again; bad depression, anxiety, fatigue, and dizzy spells came back. I had thrown off my body's balance somehow by the extra exercise and it upset me. I speculated on other disorders that might be causing my distress. It was so discouraging to sense something was wrong again and not know what it was!

I decided to turn to the Lord instead of calling more doctors. I prayed and read the scriptures, which all seemed to suggest to me that if I had faith I could be healed. When I read D&C 42:43, "And whosoever among you are sick, and have not faith to be healed, but believe, shall be nourished with all tenderness, with herbs and mild food, and that not by the hand of an enemy," it was as if the Lord was challenging me to have the faith enough to heal. He was saying, "If you don't have faith to be healed that's OK. I still love you. Just keep eating the best you know how. I know you at least believe diet is affecting you, but you'll never be healed until you have faith to change."

I had to drum up the courage to take my dad and husband off guard, so they couldn't premeditate what to say, and ask them for a healing blessing. I wanted to show the Lord I had perfect faith to be healed since I'd done "everything" in my power that I could think of to help myself.

So I did. Dad blessed me to continue learning and finding knowledge on how to heal. I was disappointed. I don't know what I was expecting but despite my best efforts at showing faith, I wasn't miraculously healed. I was just as tired, dizzy and anxious that day as ever. I felt dumb for thinking I wouldn't be.

The next day a lady in our neighborhood called me out of the blue and said she admired me not giving treats at choir practice. She asked me if she could bring me a book and send me some quotes. I agreed, and she brought me *Sugar Blues* by William Dufty. I threw it on my dresser, exhausted at the thought of opening that book. I thought, "Oh good, another anti-sugar extremist! I'll have to read through all his over-generalizing garbage to weed out the truth. I don't know if I'll even read it." I didn't look at it for three days.

Every night after the blessing I was tormented by thoughts of how foolish I was to think I could be healed. So I sent my dad an email thanking him for the blessing. I told him that I thought the Lord wasn't healing me because there was still something I could do to heal myself, but I didn't know what that was. Dad said, "I feel that He can heal you from the knowledge that he will send you. I believe He will soon." Immediately, the book my neighbor gave me entered my mind. I thought, "Was that the knowledge?" The timing was too impeccable to ignore.

I spent the whole morning reading *Sugar Blues.* Admittedly, I skimmed a lot of the historical sections. What I did read seemed unbelievable, yet the Spirit was telling me, "It is true." One quote in particular jumped off the page: "It is quite possible to improve your disposition, increase your efficiency, and change your personality for the better. The way to do it is to avoid sugar in all forms and guises."[10]

---

[10] Quote by John Tinterra taken by William Dufty in *Sugar Blues,* Grand central Life and Style Publishing, March 1986.

I had an epiphany: what if sugars weren't just exacerbating my already existing mystery illness, they were *causing* it! Overt sugar (obviously sweet and high in sugar content) I had eliminated; covert sugar (hidden or disguised as refined processed foods) were still affecting me negatively. I didn't understand how, but I felt the Holy Ghost confirm that for me sugar/refined food was the culprit. Theoretically, I would be in the state of perfect health my doctor kept claiming I should be in if I eliminated covert sugars.

April 1, 2014 I pledged to be "sugar free for life." I didn't care how hard it was this time. I would be 100% sugar free with religious fervor, even if it meant tuna forever. I couldn't have been more sure that God have given me an answer than if He had come down and told me face to face. I started a blog. I told my friends and family. I wanted to share what wonderful knowledge God had given me. I even compiled a recipe book of no sugar recipes! I was going to be healed.

I went through two days of withdrawal symptoms—cravings, tremors, and hunger after I'd just eaten. Since I'd already eliminated overt sugar, many cognitive coping tools were in place to deal with the symptoms of withdrawing from covert sugar. I didn't have one more dizzy spell after April 1. This was a sign to me the treatment was working.

I bought books to help me know what to cook, what to buy, and how to detox my system effectively. I spent a lot of time training myself to cook my own food. Thankfully, that year I had a very low client load so I was able to spend time learning the art of cooking.

However, this wasn't a quick process, and my passion started to wane by the fall. After the physical withdrawals, I had emotional withdrawals. "Why me? It's not fair! Why is it OK for everyone else and not for me? And if it's not OK for everyone else, why hasn't God commanded us to back off sugar?" Yet every time I doubted my resolve, the scriptures sent me another answer that I was on the right track: "Your body is a temple. You are keeping it clean. I forgive you your sins. Some miracles take time."

My kids struggled not having the grains and sugars they were accustomed to in the house. It was emotionally difficult feeling like I was depriving them. I came up against resistance from my spouse, my family, my friends, and my distant relatives! Nobody seemed to understand.

And then there were the problems. It seemed every negative health problem I fixed was replaced with a new problem. My body chemistry changed, and as I increased my protein and healthy fat consumption I experienced more negative symptoms of irritable bowel syndrome.

I went to a different doctor that summer because intense abdominal pain prevented me from moving. Blood work indicated that my lipase was elevated, so the doctor told me I was suffering from pancreatitis. He told me to stop eating fat and drink sprite. (Ahh, sugar!) I wasn't about to do that, so he told me to go on a juice fast for three days. I was down to eating nothing but homemade juice and lost more weight.

The pain came back every month for four months. I went back to the doctor, he had an ultrasound ordered, and we found an ovarian cyst. He said, "Never mind about the pancreatitis, nothing you can do but wait for the cyst to burst." Shortly after, I sliced my hand open because I was in the kitchen so much—back to the doctor to get fourteen stitches. Pain seemed to be my friend.

Psychologically I didn't understand why after doing so much to keep my health good, I was still suffering. In my weak moments I felt forsaken. All I did was cook, clean, and research nutrition, and in my impatience I couldn't see any fruit of my labor. I decided on our trip to Jerusalem in October 2014 I would just relax and eat what was served me. Maybe I'd have bloating or diarrhea, but food couldn't kill me, right?

It didn't kill me, but I experienced the worst abdominal pain of my life on that trip (in the middle of the night, in a foreign country). I thought I was going to die. A doctor on the trip with us told me I just had constipation and to take a laxative. I didn't believe him. I thought it was pancreatitis after all. Once we got home I went back to the doctor. He ordered many tests to rule things out, MRI, endoscope, stool tests, then referred me to a gastroenterologist.

The gastroenterologist's diagnosis: you have IBS; stop eating fat and take probiotics. He gave me no enlightenment on what caused the IBS, asked no questions about my history; he simply diagnosed what my symptoms suggested and gave a pat answer.

I had to eliminate fat *and* sugar, the two things that make food taste good. I started to *hate* food! Spending so much time trying to figure out what was "good" or "bad" or had nothing to do with my health (which still seemed so out of whack) was frustrating and stressful. Unfortunately eating was no longer pleasurable, just something I had to do.

But I didn't give up. More learning seemed to be what the Lord wanted me to do. I focused on researching what I didn't understand when I started this resolve and what the doctors couldn't answer: how digestion worked and why food had been causing my individual problems.

In combination with this knowledge, the final step in healing was to stop stressing about it. After a month of eating whole foods, limiting certain fats, writing what I was grateful for each day, and repeating "I accept God's will for my life and this body," I noticed lasting change. In February 2015, nine months after my decision to ask in faith for a healing blessing, I felt healed. Time to heal, in combination with learning and relaxation, seemed to seal my positive efforts to find a healthful diet.

What a difference 2015 was! Though still susceptible to pain and illness just as we all are, I'd nonetheless reclaimed my health and vitality in numerous ways. Having achieved some balance with my health limitations, I incorporated more carbohydrates back into my diet. I set my boundaries, learned where I could be flexible, and at what times my body's needs changed. I didn't feel deprived or confused once my relationship with food was healthy.

I have had to keep learning, evolving, and listening to my body and the direction of the Spirit. Now I feel I'm in a position where I can share this story with others because I found a way to eat wisely, in moderation and balance, aware of the food ills that create problems and equipped with the tools to overcome these problems. I fervently hope you can benefit from these tools as well.

Chapter 1; Food Awareness

You can find nutritional information almost anywhere. Nutritional wisdom, though, is rare. There is no single perfect diet but many."
Marc David

Gathering Knowledge

German philosopher Nietzsche stated that "He who has a *why* to live can bear almost any *how*."[11] You can do amazing things if you have a compelling reason to do so. Having a compelling "why" can turn strong negative emotions into strong positive emotions that keep you moving forward, just as the answer to my blessing helped me change my diet lifestyle. When it was God suggesting it, the *why* helped me endure the *how*.

Thus the challenge at this step is simply to educate yourself in order to build on *why* change needs to happen. We live in an information age. Anyone can be an expert about anything they want if they work for it and can weed out the false information.[12] Gone are the days when social class, gender, race, or religion potentially limit a person in what they want to learn. You can even find ways to learn without spending too much money.

At this point, you are likely in a preparation stage of change. You may be tempted to jump to action stage and start changing your diet now, but you need to prepare first in order for your change to be most successful. Gain a strong foundation of the meaning and purpose behind your change before you start. Reading this and other books about food, your biology, and psychology is part of your preparation.

---

[11] Taken from Viktor Frankl's work *Man's Search for Meaning*
[12] Jonny Bowden, paraphrased, author of several books on health and nutrition, jonnybowden.com

The first step in overcoming food corruptions of our day is to know what the food corruptions are. I could probably write an entire book on the topics this chapter covers alone, but that's *not* this book! Scientists and nutritionists have written that one. This book is about how to regain your spiritual, mental, and physical stamina, no matter what is ailing you, through eating delicious, healthful foods, with a positive healthy attitude about eating.

I am a mental health professional, and equipped to give you cognitive tools to aide in mental and behavioral change, which comes in handy in a diet lifestyle change. As I am not a doctor, medical practitioner, nutritionist, or dietician I cannot give you expertise on the science of biology or food. However, I can give you brief summaries on the science of what may be potentially causing problems and refer you to the expert(s) to learn more. Before we get farther into my program, this information may be crucial to understand.

Numbers at the end of the sentence indicate the foot note reference, which will provide the name and website of the experts heavily referred to. You have read my experience. I now encourage you to read others' experiences and glean the truth from what they have learned.

The Truths

If you have already started learning about food, nutrition, and diet, you probably have noticed that for thirty or so years we have been bombarded with information regarding health. In all that information are a lot of contradictions in what friends, media, professionals, and experts say. Each has research to back them up, a program for optimal health and weight loss, and advice on what, how, and when to eat.

It can be frustrating to know what to do with so many people's opinions out there. I find this particularly frustrating. One author says, "Eat all the spinach you can every day!" and another author says, "Raw spinach is toxic." Some believe dairy is acidic, an allergen, and not fit for human consumption. Others believe dairy from hormone-free and grass-fed cows is rich in dietary benefits. Some say eat green bananas for alkaline content. Others say ripe bananas are easier to digest. One expert says to take several strains of probiotics; another says we don't know what we are doing with probiotics yet, and on and on.

The truth I have weeded out from the information I've gathered is three fold:

1. Everyone has a different metabolic type and will have different dietary needs at different times in their lives.

2. There is no ONE RIGHT DIET for everyone nor is there a PERFECT diet for you.

3. In the last days, a myriad of food corruptions causing mental, physical, and spiritual health problems needs to be confronted.

The first two points are easy to accept as truth. The third point—food corruptions and pollutions abound—may be more difficult. But if you are reading this book you have a suspicion that the third point is also true. I gave the example in my story of excess sugar as a food corruption, but that does not mean sugar is "bad." Sugar has a purpose to make food desirable. The issues have become the way sugar is made, the ways we eat it, the amounts we eat, the attitude we have when we eat it, the voids we use sugar to fill, and the timing at which we eat it. This is a multifaceted problem that must be seen for what it is before it can be combated.

This program is not about eliminating foods that are corrupt, otherwise you would be eliminating everything and eating nothing. This is about making wise food choices by knowing what the corruptions are. I don't want to scare you from eating. In fact, my intention is to bring love and appreciation for food back in your life. I outline what has gone wrong in how we eat, and our individual and collective thinking about food, in order to show that there is something we can do to fix the problems.

Food and Our Body

Today toxins and environmental stress bombard us, and we only have a few ways to deal with these assaults.[13] More people are getting sick, our children are projected to die sooner than us, and our bodies response mechanism (inflammation) is responding so much that it causes tissue dysfunction and intolerance like never before in history. There are too many insults coming into our systems.

Over-consumption of sugar and refined grains is one of the food insults due to what it does to our blood sugar regulation and neurotransmitter production. Other insults are Bt toxins in genetically modified organisms (grains, produce, and animal feed); man-made sugar like high fructose corn syrup, artificial sweeteners, man-made preservatives and pesticides; higher concentration of gluten in our wheat; high concentration of unhealthy fats in meals; mercury in fish; and manmade chemicals and dyes in food and hygiene products. All these corruptions require a detoxifying action in our bodies.[14]

In addition, we have less exposure to healthy bacterial strains in gardens and fermented foods, and more exposure to man-made antibiotics. Add to these the high-paced stress of modern lifestyles with limited time to prepare, rest, and digest, and you have a perfect storm for body break down.

As if that were not enough, we have negative body image problems and judgmental people vilifying food and complicating the digestive response. When we eat in fear, we undermine our ability to optimally assimilate food.[15]

---

[13] Tom O'Bryan, DC, CCN, DACBN. "Extinguishing Inflammation: Putting out the Fire with Real Foods", www.thedr.com

[14] Tom O'Bryan, DC, CCN, DACBN. Expert on Digestion and Inflammation. Host of "The Gluten Summit" and "Abundant Energy Summit" www.thedr.com

[15] Marc David, *Nourishing Wisdom* and *The Slow Down Diet*

Gut to Brain Axis

Understanding connections between our brain and our gut can help answer why we are breaking down under the strain of food corruptions. Let's explore how diet affects blood glucose regulation and how this affects the brain. I specifically am interested in helping you understand how the evolution of food from what it used to be (a mechanism to maintain balance between gut and brain to enhance blood sugar regulation) to what it has become (an insult to our system) will give some enlightenment on food insults.

I sometimes have children clients struggling with mood dysregulation, inattention problems, or behavioral problems, and the parents are usually seeking my assistance in getting their children under control and

> *"We've come full circle, because we've known that food relates to every aspect of human health including the brain for a couple thousand years. It's only been in the past hundred years or so that the brain was looked upon as being apart from the body, as segregated from the body and that the answer to all of our maladies had to come in the form of a prescription pad. What a time it is that we're taking a step back and gaining this perspective that we always had, but unfortunately, we lost." –Dr. David Perlmutter*

advice about medication. The first thing I ask the parents about is the child's diet. For children, food is medicine, and what they eat may contribute to their life being out of control. Child psychologist Lynne Kenny said that in between behavior and medication are neurotransmitters, which are first produced in the gut. If those neurotransmitters are out of balance, a child will indicate this through misbehavior, inattention, or strong emotions.[16] Sometimes

---

[16] Lynne Kenney, Psy D. "Self Regulation: 15 Solutions for Children 3-15"

medication is important, but if you can balance these neurotransmitters through diet first, it won't be necessary to medicate the child.

A dysfunction in the brain may well cause dysfunction in the gut, and vice versa.[17] This is because the vagus nerve, located in the frontal lobe of the brain, interfaces with nervous system control of the heart and digestive tract. One example of this connection is when the nervous system is in a sympathetic state—the body does not rest and digest but rather prepares the body to fight, fly, or freeze. This is due to the vagus nerve perceiving a threat. This can pose a problem in a modern world when we are daily confronted with stresses or "threats." I have yet to meet a child suffering from anxiety that is not also suffering from either stomach problems or headaches or both.

Neurotransmitters are chemicals from our cells that transmit signals from one nerve cell to another in our brain.[18] Many neurotransmitters are synthesized from amino acids, which are readily available from the diet. Thus neurotransmitters such as glutamate, serotonin, GABA, norepinephrine, acetocholyne, dopamine, are first created in our gut, and they all need to be in balance with each other to help a brain work well.[19] Our two brains—the one in our head and the one in our bowel—must cooperate. If they do not, then there is chaos in the gut and misery in the head.

Problems in Digestion Indicate Problems in the Brain

When I refrain from eating sugar, my grandma loves to tell me, "My policy is eat dessert first!" Yes, Grandma, you have lived a long life and yes, you've eaten a lot of sugar, refined flour, and unhealthy

---

[17] Dr. Datis Kharrazian, DHSc, DC, MS. *The Gut-Brain Axis: How to Train Your Brain for Better Bowel Movements,* www.drknews.com
[18] See Wikipedia "Neurotransmitters"
[19] Leslie Korn, pHD Behavioral Medicine. "Nutrition and Mental Health" lecture, www.drlesliekorn.com

fats. You also have dementia and short term memory loss, are on several medications to keep your body functioning, have suffered from allergies all your life, and can barely walk anymore.

One could argue that all has to do with natural aging; I would add it has to do with breaking down at your weak link due to environmental insults.[20] Grandma was born before the contamination to food really got off the ground, so she had a good foundation. But she fell prey eventually. She never seemed to have any problems regulating her emotions; however, my most intelligent Grandma with her impressive vocabulary, master's degree, and sharp memory eventually lost the capacity of her short-term memory function. Many elderly people today share this problem.

What might be going awry in grandma's digestion that caused her brain to suffer? Diet affects blood chemistry, blood chemistry affects the brain cells just as it affects all cells, and brain cells are particularly vulnerable.[21] Let us not ignore the role nutrition plays in brain function. The management of blood sugar, keeping toxins out of the gut, and eating foods that are nutrient dense and whole is vitally important in both brain and body health.[22]

For example, dementia, Alzheimer's, and Parkinson's diseases are neurodegenerations now classified as a type III diabetes because of the relationship they have with the management of blood sugar, particularly in our brain.[23] Low blood sugar and high inflammation cause low brain-derived neurotrophic factor (BDNF), the connective

---

[20] On problems related to brain health and nutrition, see Steven Geanopulos "The Pain Relief Project", *Nutrient Power: Heal Your Biochemistry and Heal Your Brain* by William J. Walsh, or *The Brain Diet: The Connection between Nutrition, Mental Health, and Intelligence* by Alan Logan.

[21] See *Sugar Blues* by William Dufty

[22] Logan, Alan. *The Brain Diet: The Connection Between Nutrition Mental Health, and Intelligence*, p. 1-20. New York: Cumberland House Publishing, 2007.

[23] Dr. Steven Geanopolus www.newheightschiropractic.com

tonic in our brains that protect neurons from damage.[24] I'm sad no one told my grandma how to protect her BDNF so she could have her short-term memory even in her last years on earth.

Basic Digestion

"Blood sugar" is not sugar the way we think of it. It is actually glucose, the basic source of energy and fuel for our body. Your mouth is where digestion begins; when you smell or look at food your saliva is activated, and enzymes in your saliva begin the food breakdown process the moment you take a bite.

Simple molecules like carbohydrates (potatoes, corn, fruit, etc.) are broken down quickly by enzymes in your saliva and stomach. Large molecules like proteins and fats (meat, beans, oils) need stomach acid to break them down and perform gluconeogenesis (metabolic pathway that results in the generation of glucose from non-carbohydrate carbon substrates) to extract the glucose from these cells before enzymes can prepare them for absorption.[25]

Stomach Acid

Stomach acid needs to be high for unlocking perfect digestion.[26] For example, the pH of our food has to be right in order for other functions like bile production, pancreatic enzymes, and break down of vitamins B, A, and D to work effectively. Digesting fat is impossible without stomach acid, because without it food molecules will rot in the gut and the pH will be off when they enter the small intestines, causing problems like "leaky gut."

Vitamins and glucose are bound by protein; both have to be unbound, and the stomach acid aides in this. Bones need minerals. If the pH of your food is too high (when acid is too low), the body is

---

[24] Dr. David Perlmutter, from Underground Wellness lecture on his book *Brain Maker*
[25] Taken from *Grain Brain by* Dr. David Perlmutter, MD, www.drperlmutter.com
[26] Steven Geanopulos "The Pain Relief Project"

unable to absorb those minerals and not only bones but future
stomach acid production will suffer. Some people move to
a vegetarian diet when they feel discomfort eating proteins. It is not
because protein is bad for them, it may be that a distressed digestive
system from over consumption of toxins (and acid blocking drugs)
has interfered with proper digestion.[27]

Our intake has a lot to do with the imbalance in stomach acid
and deficiencies in enzyme and bile production. Modifying the diet
to get rid of foods that interfere with stomach acid production such
as sugar, alcohol, and caffeine, and incorporating mindful eating
practices, (such as chewing of food) will increase stomach acid and
help address this problem.[28]

Insulin

Insulin's actual job is to be your energy storage hormone. Cells
don't just take in glucose passing by them in the blood. The sugar
molecule has to be allowed into the cell by the hormone insulin.
Insulin is produced by the pancreas, and its job is to escort glucose
from the bloodstream into muscle, fat, and liver cells where it can be
used as fuel. Normal, healthy cells have a high sensitivity to insulin;
however, when we over consume hyper-processed foods filled with
refined sugars that spike insulin, our cells are exposed to high levels
of insulin, and the result is insulin resistance.[29]

Our cells adapt by reducing the number of receptors on their
surface to respond to insulin which allows cells to ignore the insulin
and fail to retrieve glucose from the blood. The pancreas then has to
respond by pumping out more insulin, so a cyclical problem is
created and can very easily culminate into type II diabetes.

---

[27] Kelly Brogan MD, Holistic Women's Health Psychiatry,
kellybroganmd.com
[28] Dr. Shawn Soszka: "The gut mood connection, how digestive problems
cause depression and anxiety"
[29] Dr. David Perlmutter, MD. *Grain Brain,* www.drdavidperlmutter.com

Furthermore, insulin is also an anabolic hormone, meaning it stimulates growth, promotes fat formation and retention, and encourages inflammation. When insulin levels are high, other hormones can be affected adversely, either increased or decreased due to insulin's constant presence. This in turn plunges the body further into unhealthy patterns of chaos that cripple its ability to recover its normal metabolism.[30] Over taxing the pancreas and causing an imbalance in insulin wreaks havoc on all other digestive processes, because of the gut to brain connection and the effect hormones have on digestion.

Obesity

Obesity is an outward indication that something inside is out of balance. There are many health problems associated with obesity, but some people don't seem to mind being overweight. I'm less concerned about the size of your waist and more concerned about the level of your pain, the cleanliness of your organs, the health of your cells, and the efficacy of your hormones. Nutritionist Diane Sanfilippo says, "As you eat more and more carbohydrates, your body responds with more and more insulin to help store that glucose for later use. There's a catch though: your body has limited storage space for carbohydrates."[31] Once the muscles and liver have stored all they can, fat cells are created to store the rest. Many have fought the battle of moderating their intake to offset storage of fat cells that add strain to other bodily functions.

Obesity is associated with many health problems because food choices impact the blood sugar-regulating hormones such as insulin, glucagon, leptin, and others. From health challenges like acne, hypothyroidism, polycystic ovarian syndrome, low testosterone, or even fertility complications to mood swings, painful periods, or

---

[30] Dr. David Perlmutter, MD. *Grain Brain,* www.drdavidperlmutter.com
[31] On carbohydrates and obesity, see Diane Sanfilippo, nutritionist. *21 Day Sugar Detox,* www.balancedbites.com

menopause, getting blood sugar regulation under control is the first step in recovery. If blood sugar regulation is not working properly, then the rest of your hormonal balance will suffer, and blood sugar regulation gets thrown out of whack when we over-consume carbohydrates and sugar.[32]

Leptin

One hormone in particular that is affected negatively by sugar consumption is leptin. Medical doctor and nutrition expert Dr. Lustig explains: "Leptin is a hormone that controls mammalian metabolism. Most people think that is the job of the thyroid, but leptin actually controls the thyroid, which regulates the rate of metabolism. Leptin

Signs of Leptin Resistance:

- being overweight
- being unable to lose weight or keep weight off
- constantly craving "comfort foods"
- fatigue after meals
- feeling consistently anxious or stressed out
- feeling hungry at odd hours of the day or night
- having a tendency to snack after meals
- having osteoporosis
- having problems falling or staying asleep
- high blood pressure
- regularly craving sugar

oversees all energy stores. Leptin decides whether to make us hungry and store more fat or to burn fat. Leptin orchestrates our

---

[32] Diane Sanfilippo, nutritionist. *21 Day Sugar Detox,* www.balancedbites.com

inflammatory response and can even control sympathetic versus parasympathetic arousal in the nervous system."[33]

Getting leptin under control will help all other hormone processes work effectively. Leptin and insulin have some things in common. They are both high in the body's chain of command, so imbalances in either tend to negatively influence every other system of the body. Leptin and insulin are themselves negatively influenced by similar things, mainly carbohydrates.

Above we discussed how continuous carbohydrate or sugar abuse on the body affects insulin pumping and will eventually lead to insulin resistance. Well the same happens with leptin. "When the body is overloaded and overwhelmed by substances that cause continuous surges of leptin, the receptors for leptin start to turn off and you become leptin resistant."[34] Meaning, even though leptin is elevated it won't work right, it won't signal to your brain that you are full so you can stop eating, and you will be less able to control your appetite, which puts you at greater risk for weight gain, which puts you at risk for brain dysfunction.

Blood Sugar Regulation

Having too high or too low glucose in the blood is toxic, which is why our bodies are designed to moderate this risk. When you eat something (usually containing some form of carbohydrate) your blood glucose rises, signaling the pancreas to release insulin commensurate with the rise in blood glucose. Insulin then tops off the liver's energy reserve by making liver starch (called glycogen) and shunts any amino acids from the blood into muscle cells. Blood sugar cannot be regulated properly without appropriate insulin responses.

---

[33] Dr. Robert Lustig *Fat Chance,* www.responsiblefoods.org
[34] On leptin, see Dr. Robert H. Lustig, MD American pediatric endocrinologist at the University of California, San Francisco where he is a professor of clinical pediatrics.

There is no energy storage without insulin—it is what allows fat cells to let energy enter and subsequently be stored as fat. The problem is if our bodies are insulin resistant from over taxing the pancreas, we start experiencing weird problems like "sugar crashes" and "hunger" even when we have a lot of fat stored in the body.[35] Spiking your insulin creates a risk of insulin absorbing too much glucose too fast, which results in low blood sugar later (symptoms include headaches, trembling or shaking, irritability, etc). When the pancreas has had enough and can't create enough insulin fast enough anymore, you risk being too high in blood sugar which results in diabetes-like health problems, (symptoms like dehydration from detoxifying the body of sugars, obesity, kidney failure, etc).

Throwing off our blood sugar regulation, insulin resistance, and leptin signals by ingesting too much sugar and refined carbohydrates also negatively affects other hormones that control the absorption, storage, and processing of our foods. Knowing what we know about the connection between the gut and the brain, we understand that all hormones—whether regulated in the brain or the gut—can be negatively affected by poor diet, specifically overconsumption of sugar. No wonder there is such a high correlation between obesity and physical maladies such as heart problems, mood problems, lower motivation, and even lower intelligence.

Other Over Eating Problems

Excessively eating sugar is like any other addiction. It feels good in the moment but long term it causes a lot of problems. Marc David notes that the need for the sweet experience is inborn, but as every nutritional scientist knows, there is no physiological requirement for refined sugar in the diet.[36] He states,

> "Quite the contrary. Excess sugar in the diet promotes tooth decay and obesity and has been implicated in heart disease,

---

[35] See Dr. David Perlmutter, MD. *Grain Brain,* www.drdavidperlmutter.com
[36] Marc David and William Dufty both use this quote.

diabetes, hypoglycemia, immune deficiency diseases, digestive disorders, and allergies. Perhaps the most fascinating and best kept medical secret about sugar is that excessive consumption causes calcium loss, which leads to a much publicized disease of our day—osteoporosis."[37]
The depletion of calcium to detoxify the body of sugar is just one of the many digestion issues caused by inadvertently or purposefully over-consuming sugar.

Furthermore, another part of our bodies enjoy sugar: our bacteria. We have an abundance of healthy bacteria in our body, that we need to survive. We also have traces of unhealthy bacteria. For example, Candida (an unhealthy strain of opportunistic bacteria)[38] will cause yeast problems, infections, inflammatory bowel disease, and lowered immune function when fed abundant amounts sugar.[39]

Evolution of Food

I've observed that there are a number of reasons why carbohydrates today are more toxic and causing more problems than they were 150 years ago. Three of those reasons include:

1. The move away from whole foods and move towards convenience.

2. The general over consumption of convenience foods.

3. The fact that man is trying to create food.

The way nature made food is the way it was intended to be ingested. Once its structure is changed, even at times by cooking, food is no longer food in a form that will be most fit for consumption, and it will create side effects. I'm referring less to cooked foods and more about food that has been processed,

---

[37] Marc David *Nourishing Wisdom*
[38] Christi Orecchio, nutritionist, twjcandidacleanse.org. Candida: any of the yeast like fungi constituting the genus CANDIDA, members of which may cause athletes food, vaginitis, thrush, or other infections.
[39] Taken from lecture by Dr. Michael Ruscio, "Solving Diarrhea"

packaged, genetically modified, even changed down to the molecular structure. The point is, if something as simple as charring your food or adding microwave radiation changes it to something that can potentially be toxic, then we ought to be careful about the way our food is grown, processed, and packaged. The way God created food is the way the body was intended to eat it.

Whole foods have sugar (fructose/sucrose) in them, so it can be safely asserted that sugar is not "bad." Food becomes corrupt when we remove the parts of the food designed to help digest the sugar. The body is designed to handle a few insults. However, in the past forty years, those insults have become so numerous that our cells are suffering, and the weakest most vulnerable cells—your genetic weak link—will eventually break down.

Alarmingly, scientists are changing the structure of seeds, modifying crops for highest yield, and changing and creating sweeteners (i.e. corn syrup).[40] Knowing how complex and delicate the inner workings of the body and mind are, and how many connections exist between all the systems, it is understandable that this may cause problems. God created our bodies, and He created the food designed for our bodies. When humans start to change the food God has created, our bodies either adapt or fall apart. Let's show some love for food by eating it as it was created, and it will show some love for us by being gentle on our bodies.

Spiritual Principle 1: Pray and Gather Knowledge

I once heard at a mental health conference that the spiritual centers of our brain are thought to be located in the prefrontal cortex or intelligence centers of our brain. This means that if you have a spiritual experience, a brain-imaging scan would pick up on it in the prefrontal cortex, rather than the amygdala hippocampus area where emotions are processed. Specifically in meditation, the left prefrontal cortex is fired, strengthening control over emotions, which may be

---

[40] See Wikipedia "corn syrup" https://en.wikipedia.org/wiki/Corn_syrup

why meditation practices have been so powerful for eons of time.[41] This suggests that when we are thinking with our emotional brain we are most likely not in tune with the Spirit.

I realize we often have strong emotions when we have a spiritual experience. I myself have had spiritual experiences so strong that I could do nothing but cry. The above concept suggests that the Spirit works in the part of the brain that sets us apart from the animals and makes us more like God—our logical brain, rather than our more primitive emotional brain. This also suggests that generally when we are having a negative emotion, the spiritual centers in our brain are not being fired. This could be why we are more vulnerable to Satan's snares and temptations when we are feeling negative emotionally.

It becomes difficult to have positive emotions when you are suffering or in pain. If you have ever experienced some kind of long term injury or intense, prolonged emotional pain, you know that at first you can take it in stride and put on a happy face for others. As time wears on, this becomes increasingly more difficult. If you are throwing off your body's metabolism by over-consuming unhealthy food, taxing your body with an array of insults, you will suffer some kind of physical or emotional pain. Feel that pain long enough and your spirituality will suffer as well.

In D&C 88:40 it states, "Intelligence cleaveth unto intelligence, wisdom receiveth wisdom; truth embraces truth; virtue loveth virtue; light cleaveth unto light." It is important for us to cleave unto, embrace, love, and receive intelligence, wisdom, truth, and light. As we do so we are increasing our spiritual centers of the brain in the prefrontal cortex! Take time to educate yourself on food corruptions and how this may affect your physical, mental, and spiritual health. This will protect your brain and the spiritual centers therein, give you more access to the Spirit, and more power over the adversary.

---

[41] http://www.crystalinks.com/medbrain.html

For example, I had a client who came in to see me because she woke up every day with a heavy feeling of depression. She had been seeing another therapist for a while and learned a lot of great cognitive behavioral therapy techniques. Despite her willingness to learn and incorporate these principles in her life she still felt mildly depressed so the therapist referred her to me, thinking maybe a female would be a better fit for her.

I let her spend quite a bit of time telling me her past and current situation, and asked her if she would be willing to try a diet change. She didn't see how that would do anything, but she agreed. Together we came up with a realistic, whole food diet that cut out many sugary and refined foods, and her assignment was to implement it.

I didn't see her again for a few weeks and wondered if I would never see her again because I tried to tell her what to eat. Thankfully, about a month later she came in for a follow up to let me know that she hadn't rescheduled because the diet change completely worked and she no longer felt depressed.

Even knowing what I did about food, I was surprised. After years of feeling mildly depressed every morning, just tweaking her diet completely got rid of it? She reported that as long as she cooked her own food and stayed away from treats she felt great, and she was coming in for advice because her new job at a summer camp required her to eat the cafeteria food and she wasn't sure what to do.

I was amazed! Here was another person who had experienced a remarkable positive change in mood due to eating wisely. She had taken a brave step towards claiming not only physical health, but also mental health, which lessened her pain, thereby increasing potential for spiritual connection and potential.

The story doesn't end well, due to certain environmental forces she wasn't able to keep at it and the depression returned. But I have hope for her that she will remember this helped, try it again in the future, and stick to it—that's a wise food mind.

Challenge 1: Learn

And as all have not faith, seek ye diligently and teach one another words of wisdom; yea, seek ye out of the best books words of wisdom; seek learning, even by study and also by faith. —*Doctrine and Covenants 88:118*

In summary, I've given you a teaser about the abundance of information regarding nutrition and diet. I used overconsumption of sugar as an example because it is one of the biggest, if not the biggest, food insult of our day. But there are many others: stressful eating, food addictions, eating with negative feelings about food and self, inflammatory foods, antibiotics, pesticides, hormones, trans fats, etc. There is a need for the general population to learn what those food corruptions are so we can take wise steps to protect our intake. Ponder these questions:

- ✓ Is there anything that you have suffered that may have been exacerbated by unhealthy eating or food insults?
- ✓ When you think about eliminating food corruptions and changing your relationship with food, what benefit in your life comes to mind?
- ✓ Have you heard stories of others being healed or cleansed by changing their food habits, but just don't know where to start?

Here is where to start: learn *what are food corruptions in my life?* Books you might like that help understand the evolution of food and its corruptions are listed in the resources section at the end of the book. Choose some to read and help you learn what might be affecting your health.

If you'd prefer not to read another book, you can watch lectures about what others have discovered about food and our nation's health and mental health problems (youtube.com). My three favorite lectures are "Liberate yourself from nutritional confusion,"[42] "Sugar

---

[42] https://www.youtube.com/watch?v=5AKZWneNhnA

Is Killing Us,"[43] and "The Bitter Truth."[44] The Fed Up documentary[45] is also a great resource. Listen to the Spirit and weed out the inaccuracies.

Eating well is an investment on your brain and gut health. Though it may take time, health improves with consistent healthy eating. You can go to my website and click on the resources link to learn more (www.wisefoodmind.com). When you feel some of the confusion has been answered, go on to the next step, "Observe Inside Forces."

---

[43] https://www.youtube.com/watch?v=Yda8RtOcVFU
[44] https://www.youtube.com/watch?v=dBnniua6-oM
[45] *Fed Up Documentary*, with Katie Couric. Directed by Stephanie Soechtig. Anchor Bay Studios, 2014.

Chapter 2: Observe Inside Forces

The purpose of our lives is not just the building of beautiful bodies,
but perfecting and refining our divine spirit and becoming more
God-like.

Paavo Airola[46]

Four Realms of Human Experience

Think of your human experience as comprising four realms:
spiritual, biological, psychological, and environmental/social. Inside
forces are biological and psychological. Outside forces, which we
will discuss in chapter three, are environmental and social.

Spiritual forces are both inside and outside, as our spirit (inside)
is connected with the spirits around us (outside), and connected to
our Heavenly Father. In *Nourishing Wisdom*, a book you may have
read in step one, Marc David counsels:

We are more than just a body, a tongue, and an assortment of
nutritional requirements. We are a soul clothed in the elements of the
earth, journeying in a realm where matter and spirit unite in human
form. We are of a spiritual source. From it we emerge at birth, and to
it we return at death. It is here in the spiritual realm that our journey
into the mind of the eater begins.[47]

When you think of eating as choosing life, and that life is the
Spirit, intervening biologically by improving diet can be seen as
intervening spiritually as well. Like a feedback loop, spiritual
principles and intervention are an integral part of wisely intervening
biologically.

Realms of Experience are Interconnected

All domains influence and affect the other; positive intervention
in one realm can help lift the others. Neglect in one realm can

---

[46] Paavo Airola, *Hypoglycemia:A better approach*
[47] Marc David, *Nourishing Wisdom,* chapter 1

negatively influence all the others. If you can imagine it like circles all connected to each other, within the circle of spiritual realm, you can get a better visual of how they are connected. This brings hope to someone who may suffer in any one aspect of his or her experience: that if you can even do one positive thing to change, it will positively affect all areas of life.

For example, you mentally tell yourself that your productivity level is tied to your self worth, which makes it feel impossible to decrease your work load. This can cause high levels of stress in your environment. This can affect your time to rest and exercise, and even may negatively affect your eating patterns. You can manage stress by monitoring your thoughts. Specifically, break down the core belief that you have to be productive to be worthwhile, which will decrease anxiety (psychological). This may increase your ability to digest food (biological), which may in turn cause you to feel better physically and improve your outlook on life (environmental). Changing thought patterns can be powerful, and is why therapy benefits people in more aspects of life than just psychology.

For some, just reading scriptures and singing hymns is enough of a positive influence to cope with the negative aspects in the other three human domains. It was enough for me until I was a young mother and my physical brain needed more help than my spiritual coping tools could provide. I spent many years working in the psychological realm by monitoring my thoughts: priorities, distortions in thinking, number of negative thoughts about myself and others, and number of positive thoughts. I did a lot of work positively influencing my psychological realm and this helped rewire my brain in many wonderful ways. However, I didn't permanently overcome my emotional problems until I intervened in the biological realm.

Positive Intervention in Biological Realm

One way to intervene in the biological realm is with healthful food. Most people already know why, how, and what they are eating causes some of their problems. So why can't we just eat better? We have many inside forces compelling us to continue eating as we have been. Marc David suggests that, "Negative habits are mechanical. We may understand exactly what is good for us and know how to eat, yet there is no guarantee we will do what is right. This is the paradoxical nature of the mind: knowing does not lead to doing. Negative habits are so mechanical that we are compelled to repeat them even when we want to stop."[48] Observing those forces is the first step in overcoming them and taking back your eating agency.

Biological inner forces that keep us eating unhealthily involve dopamine and bacteria. Psychological inner forces that do the same are habit and thinking errors, specifically all-or-nothing thinking errors about certain foods. Understanding the general drawbacks and benefits of individual foods can help us combat all-or-nothing thinking errors so we can more easily make wise food choices.

Biological Inner Forces: Bacteria

Another biological force that keeps us eating unhealthy is our microscopic bacterial flora. We are composed of millions of bacterial organisms, several different strains, and some of them are good and some of them are bad. They all have their place in our bodies, but when we over-eat unhealthy food the bad bacteria become opportunistic and multiply in places where they are not supposed to be.

Candida is an example of bacteria that can overgrow and cause many problems like yeast, fatigue, and headaches. When you have a craving for something sweet (and you have an overgrowth of Candida), it's most likely the bacteria signaling your brain to bring in more sugary food for them. You are literally feeding an organism bigger than yourself when you have an imbalance of good and bad

---

[48] Marc David *Nourishing Wisdom*

bacteria.[49] That is why probiotics have become so popular these days. With the antibiotics prevalent in our medications and food, with the over consumption of sugar, and with not enough soil-based healthy bacteria to feed on due to monoculture and modified seeds, the bad bacteria are taking over and the good guys can't give us the benefits we need.[50] Taking probiotics will help restore some balance, but not feeding the opportunistic bacteria is crucial to eliminating this problem.

Biological Inner Forces: Dopamine

Dopamine is the reward neurotransmitter. Food has been a reward and a comfort to us since infancy. Nourishment is associated with connection, i.e. mothers calm their infants with milk. We are wired with dopamine impulses from our birth to associate food with comfort. Dopamine may be the strongest biological force when it comes to eating.

A clear understanding of what inner forces compel us to do may help us accept cravings and change the cycle. For example, I sat by a lady at a lunch party one day and she said, "I have to keep candy bars in my purse because I have hypoglycemia. When I start feeling moody I know I need some sugar!"

Does her body really need sugar? What she was doing was causing even more hyper-insulinism, insulin resistance, and mood disturbances. This was perpetuating her "hypoglycemic complex," and worse, causing a vicious addiction to sugar. Just as an alcoholic needs more alcohol to feel "normal," her brain needed sugar to keep herself feeling ok. What her body needed was nourishment not achieved by candy. Dopamine was at work keeping this good woman in a negative eating cycle

---

[49] Christi Orecchio has spoken to this point in lecture series "Digestion Sessions" with Sean Croxton.
[50] Dr. Allison Siebecker, ND "How to Beat the Bloat: Small Intestine Bacterial Overgrowth"

Sugar and Dopamine

The form of the sugar is what makes it addictive. White and brown sugar are derived from sugar cane or sugar beets, both of which are whole foods that have high fiber and vitamin content when eaten whole. However, the way we have been eating cane and beet sugar for over one hundred years now is in its processed, refined, and bleached form that leaves only its sweetening benefit. This means it will process quickly in the body and will affect your brain cells. Like other drugs, it will cross the blood brain barrier. You will feel happy for a moment, then when the sugar high is over, you will crash, feel moody, and hungry.

In "Pleasure Unwoven," Kevin McCauley explains how sugar affects dopamine, the pleasure and reward neurotransmitter. He gave the example of the bubble gum machine. When you put a quarter in a bubble gum machine, you expect one bubble gum to pop out, and when it does you experience pleasure and reward. If, when you put in a quarter, for some reason *two* bubble gums pop out and you get more than you expected, you have a heightened feeling of reward and pleasure. However, if the next time you only get one gum-ball, instead of reward and pleasure you will feel disappointment.[51]

The same is true with refined sugar. When you eat something as sweet as a candy bar, the reward and pleasure (dopamine surge) is so great it heightens the hedonic pleasure centers of your brain. So the thought of eating an apple is disappointing. Whether the candy bar is good for you or not becomes a moot point. Your brain just wants the reward!

Bacteria signals and dopamine surges are why many people, even though they know they have a weight problem and probably suspect their health issues are related to diet, will resist the idea of changing their diet. Those biological forces are so intense! The idea

---

[51] Kevin McCauley "Pleasure Unwoven: a personal journey about addiction", www.instituteforaddictionstudy.com

of having pleasure now overpowers any negative consequence later. The good news is that the hedonic pleasure centers can be reset and the brain rewired with time, so that a salad with many wonderful vegetables can be extremely satisfying and rewarding as it should be. But getting to that point takes confronting a few thinking errors.

Psychological Inside Forces: Habits

The mind likes things to be predictable and controlled, and often we behave in the ways we do out of habit. Creating positive habits offset negative habits, which is why parents try to teach their children to cultivate positive habits like reading scriptures, praying daily, exercising, and doing chores. Once it is a habit, it is much easier to continue that behavior; in fact, it becomes difficult to break the habit once ingrained.

The same is true for negative behaviors. Any behavior that is done with great frequency is held in our central nervous system in much the same way as a computer stores information. Certain stimuli will access the neural patterning for that particular behavior and cause it to be fired. Every negative habit has a similar neurological triggering process. When confronted with certain stimuli (three o'clock, time for Dr. Pepper!), we are automatically drawn to substances that we associate with alleviating the pain and providing us immediate pleasure: alcohol, caffeine, sugar, etc. Habits are difficult to deal with. They are encoded in the body and are activated without conscious input.[52]

We will discuss how to break habits in great detail in later chapters. For now, observe the patterns of your eating habits. What are you in the habit of eating for breakfast? Lunch? Snacks? Dinner? When you are at work? When you visit family? It has become part of you brain's code to eat in certain ways at certain times and circumstances.

---

[52] Paraphrased from Marc David's chapter on cravings in *Nourishing Wisdom*

Psychological Inside Forces: Thinking Errors

When you are confronted with the option of eating a carrot or a piece of cake, what thoughts start to run through your head? Dopamine will be screaming at you to eat the cake, and you may be thinking such things as:

"It has grains in it. I haven't had my carbs today."

"I've had a tough day. I deserve a reward"

"One piece of cake didn't hurt anyone. Isn't it OK to have a little sugar?"

"Cake will taste better and fill me up. Food should taste good. Besides, if I eat a carrot I'll still feel hungry!"

"I don't care how I look. If people have a problem with it that's too bad"

"Granny's been eating cake every day and she has lived ninety-four years!"

Pick your favorite statement or write your own thoughts down on a piece of paper. After we discuss what thinking errors are, we will come back to your thoughts and examine some distortions that are really rationalizations for your desire to experience reward.

Top Ten Cognitive Distortions

David Burns outlines ten common cognitive distortions people use in their thought processes on a daily basis that keep them rutted in negative behaviors and perceptions.[53] These distortions are the seedbed of basing your perception on false information, or for rationalizing your own agenda, and preventing you from changing and improving. It is worth reviewing them here so that you will recognize this force when it happens.

All or Nothing (black and white thinking): this distortion assumes that if you are not perfect, you are a failure; if you are not

---

[53] On "Thinking Errors," see David D. Burns, MD *The Feeling Good Handbook*

beautiful, you are ugly; if you are not smart, you are stupid. Life does not work this way. In truth, we are both beautiful and ugly, smart and stupid, and none of us perfect but all of us successful in some way.

Overgeneralizing: seeing negative events as a never-ending pattern of defeat. You can generally catch this thinking error by noticing the words "always," "never," "nothing," "everything," "everyone," etc. This is All or Nothing thinking on repeat. "I always forget things!" or "He never listens!"

Mental Filter: only paying attention to certain types of evidence (usually negative) and ignoring the rest. This is similar to All or Nothing thinking, but in more specific ways designed to justify our own viewpoint and keeps us from substantial change, i.e. "I messed up, I should quit!"

Disqualifying the Positive: this distortion does not necessarily pay attention to any negative evidence, but does assume or insist the positive doesn't count. Another type of All or Nothing thinking, this thinking error will dismiss the positive feedback or successes you accomplish in life because it just doesn't matter for some reason.

Jumping to Conclusions (Mind Reading): assuming you know what will happen or what people are thinking. Our brains usually do this for good reason. At some time in the past you may have experienced something negative in a certain situation or with a certain type of person and so your brain warns you that this could happen again in a same situation. This can cause unnecessary anxiety and may not have any validity.

Minimizing (Denial) or Maximizing (Catasrophizing): shrinking the evidence to purport your own agenda or blowing things out of proportion. This is a type of Emotional Reasoning (coming up next) where you have an emotional desire to do or be something so you minimize the negative consequences of that behavior or maximize the positive. Or, if you feel a negative emotional reaction due to someone else's behavior, you minimize their good and maximize their faults.

Emotional Reasoning: assuming because you feel something it must be true. If your friend or spouse treated you poorly, you *feel* like they are mean, insensitive, and not worthy of your love, and assume that feeling means it is true. Or maybe you *feel* sad and depressed in the morning, so you assume that your life is dull, pointless, and maybe assume because you feel this way you must be worthless, unlovable, and unwanted.

Should Statements: saying to yourself "I should," "I must," "I ought," or "I'm supposed to" is a common cognitive distortion. Think about who decided what "should" be? Your parents? This book? (One could argue this whole book is one big should statement.) The government? God? Everyone is different, and what should be true for one may not be true for another. This is a black and white thinking error combined with emotional reasoning and topped off with a huge dose of guilt.

Labeling: using one-word descriptions of people, self, or situations thus disqualifying any other aspect of that person/situation. Examples of labeling are hurtful words like "jerk," "slut," "loser," "fat," and "stupid." This is All or Nothing thinking in its most ignorant form. When we mold ourselves or anyone else into any one description we take away the potential to change, and change is an eternal process for every person.

Personalization: all my fault or all your fault. There are many pieces of the responsibility pie, and it does no good to completely blame anyone, including ourselves. Blaming ourselves for our many trials again creates guilt, shame, and is counterproductive when it comes to change. Blaming others only creates a victim stance and also prevents change as it creates the thought that because it's others' fault, it is outside of one's control.

Thinking Errors Perpetuate Eating Habits

Let's now look at the previously outlined thoughts that may occur when a person is debating whether or not to eat a cake or a carrot and discover what thinking errors are being used.

It has grains in it. We are supposed to eat grains, and I haven't had many carbs today.

Thinking errors:

Emotional Reasoning (the fact that you haven't had an abundance of carbs today is no reason to justify eating more carbs, but the brain turns it into a reason because you are feeling an emotion—the desire to feel pleasure).

Minimizing (focusing on the one somewhat healthy ingredient and conveniently ignoring the unhealthy oils, sugars, preservatives, and coloring).

Personalization (it is the world health organization's fault, the food pyramid tells me to eat grains).

I've had a tough day. I deserve a reward.

Emotional Reasoning (finding justification through reward system of reinforcing behavior).

Minimizing (denying the fact that in the long run unhealthy food is not a reward).

Maximizing (your day was *awful* and you need something good in it).

Disqualifying the Positive (failing to recognize the good in your day and other potential rewards of your efforts).

One piece of cake didn't hurt anyone. Isn't it OK to have a little sugar?

Mental filter (only paying attention to certain types of evidence and ignoring the rest—you've already had plenty of unhealthy food, just because it wasn't cake doesn't mean you can splurge now).

Jumping to Conclusions (one piece of cake might just hurt someone).

Labeling (what is "a little sugar" anyway? I would argue that one piece of cake is A LOT of sugar).

Cake will taste better and fill me up. Food should taste good. Besides, if I eat a carrot I'll still feel hungry.

All or Nothing thinking (many healthy foods taste good).

Should Statements (who said food should taste good in order to eat it? Some of the most healing foods in the world don't taste that great).

Emotional Reasoning (unless you feel happy and satisfied the food isn't worth eating, which resembles a craving).

I don't care how I look. If people have a problem with it that's too bad.

Minimizing (paying attention to only how you gain weight is ignoring all the other problems that comes with eating unhealthily).

Disqualifying the Positive (there are other reasons to care about how you look other than what other people think of you).

Jumping to Conclusions (mind reading that others care about how you look).

Should Statements (a hidden assumption that there is some better way you "should" look, so you have to coach yourself into dismissing how "bad" you do look).

Granny's been eating cake every day and she has lived ninety-four years!

Minimization (because she does it I can do it).

Mental Filter (she may be alive, but what is her quality of life?)

One note about this last thinking error. When you filter out the positive benefits of change and hang on to one type of evidence, *that I could still have a long life*, you'll be stuck in the same behaviors with not enough reason to change. As Wendy Cook stated, "The argument that we are living longer must be qualified by the fact that longer lives are accompanied by debilitating and long-standing illnesses such as Parkinson's disease, Alzheimer's disease, arthritis, and diabetes."[54]

Have you discovered some common thinking errors of your own? They are pretty sneaky right? When I am feeling an emotional desire to eat, I find that I have a harder time combating thinking

---

[54] Wendy E. cook *Foodwise*

errors. I can come up with many rationalizations to eat the food that will give me pleasure and relief for a few minutes!

The final thinking error I want to address before moving on is this statement:

"I admire that you eat only whole foods, but I never could."

I have heard this many times! Are you saying it as well? Explore what you mean by that. What are the distortions in this statement?

Overgeneralizing (never): you could if you had to, i.e. if other options were not available.

Jumping to conclusions: change is a potential for any person.

All or Nothing: if you try and can't you have "failed." Trying is doing. We try, we fail, we try, we fail, we try again...and one day the habit is broken and we have a break through!

You can do it! Mind your mind-chatter. Replace "I never could" with a statement that has no distortions. Maybe like this:

"It is possible to train my brain to eat the way I feel is healthy for me if I work for it."

Antidotes for Thinking Errors

The Story of the Taoist Farmer[55]

Once upon a time there was a man with one acre of land, one faithful son, and one beautiful horse. One day his horse got loose and ran away, and all his family and friends said, "Oh! How unfortunate for you! That's your only horse. What are you going to do?" But the man said, "I don't know if it's a good thing or a bad thing."

The horse joined a group of wild horses and became thirsty. So he found his way back to the farm and brought ten wild horses with him. All the farmer's family and friends said, "Oh, how fortunate for you. You now have ten more horses!" The man said, "I don't know if it's a good thing or a bad thing."

---

[55] "The Story of The Taoist Farmer" as told by Chin Ning Chu in "The Asian Mind Came" New York: Macmillan Publishing Company, page 182. (1991)

One day while the man's son was out training one of the wild horses, the horse reared up and landed on the boy, and broke both his legs. The farmer's family and friends said to him, "Oh! How unfortunate for you. That's your only son. What are you going to do?"

The man said, "I don't know if it's a good thing or a bad thing."

The next week war broke out and all the able-bodied young men in the village were called to serve in the war. The farmer's son could not go due to his broken legs, and all the sons of the village were killed on the front. All the famer's friends bitterly chided, "How fortunate for you, Your son did not have to go to war." The man only replied, "I don't know if it's a good thing or a bad thing."

After some time the farmer's son became depressed because his friends had all died in the war, and he had not been able to fight with them. So he left the farm and his father to find a better life. As neighbors wondered how the farmer would be able to go on, he said "I don't know if it's a good thing or a bad thing."

Five years later the son returned with a small fortune and a wife, and the old man was able to retire. He sold his farm to his son, and he became quite wealthy. Though others looked on in envy, the wise man only smiled.

"I don't know if it's a good thing, or a bad thing."
****

I love this story because it helps us understand that there are pros and cons to any event that may happen in life, whether or not it is originally perceived as good or bad. I'm sure you can think of personal examples of this in your own life.

The idea that we don't have to sweat and slave over agriculture in our lifetimes anymore because food is mass produced and feeding millions all over the world could be perceived as a fortunate thing. But there are some drawbacks.

Observe Food Drawbacks and Benefits

There are pros and cons to every food. Even sugar has its benefit. Eating fruit and grains in their season and meats sparingly as the Word of Wisdom[56] suggests promotes a regular rhythm digestion and storing fat that is important in our lives. But now that we have every fruit and grain and meat we can think of at any season we want, there needs to be some rules of behavior for food.

I would caution you to avoid reading lists of foods you "should never eat" or "should always eat" because that is an overgeneralization (and a Should Statement) that may not be based in truth. "From day to day and season to season, the body changes in size, metabolism, energy needs."[57] And at any given time the body may be in need of a different kind of food. After much researching specific foods, I have come up with drawbacks and benefits to most of what we eat, which may help us get away from All or Nothing thinking or Should Statements.

Grass and Grains

Benefits: versatile, easy to digest, affordable and abundant

Drawbacks: cause of inflammation, modified and hybridized, refined

Example: With whole rice (brown) only the outer husks have been removed. With white rice, the germ, husk and outer layers have been removed. Polished white rich is further refined as it is passed through powerful rollers and polished with talc. Wild rice is harvested in North America and has higher levels of protein and minerals. Rice is rich with vitamin B when eaten whole. When eaten refined, it is basically a starch with few nutritional benefits, such as puffed rice. Robert Runnels said, "Man commits a crime against nature when he eats the starch from the seed and throws away the mechanism necessary for the metabolism of that starch!"[58]

---

[56] Doctrine and Covenants Section 89
[57] Quote by Marc David
[58] Quote taken from Wendy E. Cook *Foodwise*

Fruits and Vegetables

Benefits: nutrient dense, medicinal properties, vitamins and fiber

Drawbacks: Pesticides, fertilizers, FODMAP's, nightshades, added sugars

Example: Juice is medicine if you juice fruit and veggies yourself. Fresh juice helps mobilize waste in the gall bladder. Fresh juice is concentrated with vitamins, minerals and phytochemicals; however, the fiber is removed so it is a "fast carb" and there is a much higher fructose concentration. It's better for blood sugar regulation to eat the whole fruit (blended or raw). Also, as fresh juice has no preservatives, it's best to drink it or freeze it within twenty-four hours. Juice or processed fruit can be dangerous if made with added sugars, preservatives, and color dyes. Many juices in the stores have High Fructose Corn Syrup added to them.

Fat

Benefits: proper ratio of fatty acids improves brain and heart function

Drawbacks: imbalance of fatty acids and free radicals

Example: You may have heard of omega-6 fatty acids (found in vegetable oils) and omega-3 fatty acids (found in fish and eggs) that are important for our digestion. Too much omega-6 relative to omega-3 can lead to a number of inflammation-related diseases, including cardiovascular disease, which is why there has been a surge in fish oil supplements and consuming "healthy fats." Consuming vegetable oils—corn, canola, soybean oils found in salad dressings and processed foods—can tip the scale too far toward omega-6.

Furthermore, vegetable oils, including olive oil, are not heat stable and become toxic when heated to extreme temperatures. Processed oils are made in factories with high heat, which creates free radicals and trans fats. These damage cells and are associated with many health problems, from obesity to cancer to heart disease. It is no coincidence that there has been a steady increase in heart disease since processed oils were introduced in the early 1900s. Chemicals used to refined processed oils can pollute the finished product.[59]

The brain needs fat, especially children's brains for proper neurological development.[60] Healthy, stable fats such as coconut oil, avocado oil, organic butter and ghee, fish oil, and even fat and broth from lean, land roaming animals have become a popular solution to the toxic oil problem.

Meats/Protein

Benefits: amino acids, glandular nutrient dense, vitamins and minerals

Drawbacks: harder to digest, modified grain, hormones, antibiotics fed

Example: When cows ingest corn, the fatty acid composition of their meat changes from a near perfect ratio of omeg-6 and omega-3 to a twenty to one ratio. This can create inflammation in people and is the real reason why red meat may be a major contributor to heart disease, diabetes, cancer, and more. Organic, pastured, and one hundred percent grass fed animals have a balanced ration of omegas.[61]

Dairy

Benefits: vitamins and healthy fat, probiotics

Drawbacks: hormones, antibiotics, pasteurization, intolerance

Example: Cheese is processed milk fat, and its aging process

---

59 Weeks and Boumrar, "Mediterranean Paleo Cooking" and *The 21-Day Sugar Detox* by Diane Sanfilippo
60 Jonny Bowdon, in "A renegade look at nutrition" from the Future of Healing Conference.
61 On food drawbacks and benefits, see recipe book by Weeks and Boumrar, "Mediterranean Paleo Cooking"

provides benefits. Yogurt is very beneficial if homemade or made from organic, grass fed cows. Kefir is also beneficial. It's a probiotic made from kefir grains and full fat milk that gives the body a healthy balance of good bacterial strains.

Sugar

Benefits: sweetens food

Drawbacks: spikes insulin, overworks enzyme production, reduces stomach acid, elevates mood then mood crashes, heightens hedonic pleasure center, stores as fat quickly, creates free radicals, AGE products, taxes all organs.

Example: corn syrup, defined by Wikipedia as follows:

> Corn syrup is a food syrup which is made from the starch of maize and contains varying amounts of maltose and higher oligosaccharides, depending on the grade. Corn syrup is used in foods to soften texture, add volume, prevent crystallization of sugar, and enhance flavor. Corn syrup is distinct from high-fructose corn syrup (HFCS), which is manufactured from corn syrup by converting a large proportion of its glucose into fructose using the enzyme D-xylose isomerase, thus producing a sweeter compound due to higher levels of fructose.[62]

God put small traces of fructose in food to make it desirable so we could get all the other benefits of the food. When we extract the sugar so we can make food sweeter, we take away all the elements that made it something our bodies were meant to digest. Not smart. Chemically altering the corn creates an entirely different organism. So my question is, is it still a food? William Dufty said:

> The words holy, whole, and healthy all stem from the same root. A whole food is holy, intended to protect the health of man. Sugar is not a whole food... Definition of poison: any

---

[62] See wikipedia "corn syrup"

substance applied to the body, ingested, or developed within the body which causes or may cause disease. Sugar is classified as a poison because it has depleted the body of its life force, vitamins, and minerals.[63]

Unfortunately, there are no nutritional benefits to eating sugar. A person could live a lifetime and never eat an ounce of raw sugar and have all their nutritional needs met. Furthermore, the drawbacks outweigh the benefits. This could be seen as one of life's cruel ironies—that the foods most appealing are the least beneficial. The benefit is indulgence, another reason we must be aware and observant about what foods we are ingesting.

There are certainly some good things about having manmade foods, mass produced, and available to many people in the world. Remember the story of the Taoist Farmer, because in order to wisely observe forces that compel us to eat, we have to make some righteous judgments about what the food is doing to us.

Instead of thinking All or Nothing, let us consider that there might be two sides to this food culture we have been thrust into as we observe the corruptions in order to prevent us from saying to ourselves or others "how unfortunate for you."

Spiritual Principle 2: Discipline and Sacrifice

It took a lot of discipline and sacrifice for me to change. I wanted to give up many times, but I had been given so much knowledge about the foolishness of going back and so much direction of the Spirit to continue on the path I was on, I could not turn back. Realizing the principle of truth that God told Adam in the Garden of Eden, "By the sweat of thy brow thou shalt eat thy bread all the days of thy life"[64] has kept me on the wise food-eating path. I can testify to you I'm a better person for it.

---

[63] William Dufty *Sugar Blues*
[64] *Pearl of Great Price*, Moses 4:25

As we gear up to intervene positively in the biological realm, let us arm ourselves with the spiritual principles of discipline and sacrifice. Changing our perception of food as "fast and convenient" to "something worth working for" can help make a change towards a more healthful diet. I was watching a provident living video on LDS.org and a young woman living in Africa quoted 2nd Thessalonians 3:10 saying, "The hand that does not work, must not eat."[65] As you ponder changing, consider that it may take work, and that is truly a good thing.

Bread has been the staff of life from the beginning of this Earth. I learned from eating only protein and veggies for a while that it is not such a good idea. For me, it caused a lot of other problems. We need the glucose from carbohydrates. But there is a caveat: we must eat by the sweat of our brow. There is a big difference between growing wheat uncontaminated and unchanged from its original form, grinding wheat, mixing bread, waiting for it to rise, and baking it before you can actually eat it, and thirty-minute microwaveable cinnamon rolls from the freezer. As long as we are living in a fallen world, working to eat is a truth.

Ah, we have gotten clever about getting around this principle so we don't have to sweat about eating. Take caution. Those who do not "eat by the sweat of their brow" may likely be suffering consequences. Men from the time of the fall were supposed to work hard to grow the food, women were intended to work hard preparing it, and children were meant to learn from this example. Our flesh is weak otherwise. When our eating habits become corrupted, our spirituality lessens.

We can still benefit from the talents of one another. I can pay a local farmer for his eggs and milk, a local grocer for homemade pickles, and pay someone to cook my meals for me. And I am grateful they spared me all that work! But then I need to be working

[65] https://www.lds.org/media-library/video/2014-06-1940-dorothy-groundnut-paste?category=testimonials-and-stories&lang=eng

in some other area to earn that money; so work I must if I want good quality food for my body. The best way to eat is to work for it yourself. "Fast" and "food," insofar as I have been able to observe, were never meant to go together while we live on this Earth. If you are cutting out the work, you may not be eating food the way God intended.

Challenge 2: ABC Chart

For the next few days, use the following diagram (ABC chart) to write down situations when you ate food out of habit you know is not good for your health. Write down the situation (A). Write down how you felt physically or emotionally (C). Then write down the thoughts that went through your mind before and during the situation (B). Identify any thinking errors that may be keeping you stuck.

Every body is different. Do not let the cognitive Should Statement "because everyone else eats it I should be able to eat it" influence your dietary decisions. Also beware the Should Statement "I shouldn't be eating this," which causes fear, guilt, and self-loathing. Wherever you are at in this journey is fine! Let the Spirit and the observations you have made lead you. In addition to observing inside thinking patterns, write down some goals you would prefer to (not should) do about your eating habits. The Spirit will let you know what is best if you ask sincerely through prayer.

A   **B**   **C**

SITUATION   THOUGHTS   MOOD/EMOTIONS

_____

THINKING ERRORS

_____
_____
_____
_____

MY HEALTHY EATING GOALS

In 5 days_____

In 6 months_____

In 1 year_____

Questions to consider:

- What inside forces keep you stuck?
- How would things be different if you had a healthy hedonic pleasure center, and didn't associate food with reward?
- How much easier would it be if you thought about food in different ways, with no cognitive distortions justifying your behavior?
- Do you suspect any larger forces, i.e. an unhealthy bacterial strain in your gut, are at work here?
- In which ways does the Adversary tempt you the most?
- Is it possible the Spirit has been trying to warn you that certain foods are causing problems, but was being ignored?

Chapter 3: Observe Outside Forces

"It mattereth not whether the principle is popular, I will always maintain a true principle, even if I stand alone in it."

The Teachings of Joseph Smith, p. 515

Outside Forces

The word *diet* stems from the Latin root *dieta*, which means "a day's work." *Dieta* stems from the Greek work *diaita* which means "way of life."[66] I don't like to think of diet as a restriction, but rather what the root suggests, to regulate one's way of life with daily work. What is your "way of life?"

Outside forces have a lot to do with our diet, or way of life. These can often be the understated and hardest forces to contend with when trying to change. Social forces, such as being seen as the weird one or not fitting in, family traditions, practices of reinforcing children with sweets, are all social forces that keep us stuck. Environmental, historical, and political forces are nearly impossible to compete with. The spiritual force of the Adversary can make change particularly difficult.

In this step I call for an observation of outside forces and how these affect your "way of life." We live in a land of plenty. How do we control it? Overeating and food addictions can start from outside forces. In this step's challenge, you will observe how these forces affect your health by writing down what you eat and how you feel.

Social Structure, Norms, and Taboos

When I began my MSW program at BYU, I abstained from sugar for an assignment in my substance abuse class. During the first week of this assignment, the entire MSW class of 2011 and our

---

[66] http://www.etymonline.com/index.php?term=diet

spouses were invited to a catered dinner introducing the program. My husband and I sat next to two couples. One of the students sitting next to me was also in my substance abuse class and had also decided to abstain from sugar as part of his assignment.

Already sitting next to each plate was a large piece of decadent cheesecake with chocolate glaze and strawberries and raspberries on the side. I felt relieved that there was someone else at the table who would also pass up the amazing dessert.

"I just love coming to these catered dinners," I commented to my class member. "I especially love the desserts they provide. It's really too bad we won't be able to eat it this time."

He just looked at me. "Yeah, well, I've already messed up. I ate sugar yesterday."

"I know what you mean," I replied. "There is sugar in everything! I had to change my rules a little bit because I can't avoid it if it's in my dinner. But I certainly can't eat this chocolate covered cheesecake."

"No, I mean I messed up and ate candy, and some ice cream too," he said.

"Ah." I wondered what that meant for him for this assignment and if he was even taking it seriously. He half smiled, indicating that to him it really wasn't that important.

"Well," I said, "maybe you can go without it just this once and write about your experience in the paper due at the end of the month. That way I will have someone to keep me company as I refrain."

"OK, maybe."

We ate our catered meals and enjoyed the conversation. The other people around the table started to eat the dessert, and I gave mine to my husband. My dopamine started to surge as I watched him eat it. Evenings after dinner were a huge trigger for me. I wanted that dessert badly. I looked at my friend next to me. He was looking at the cheesecake, and I knew what he was battling.

"Well I can't do it, I'm eating this thing!" he said as he dove right in and enjoyed the dessert. I laughed a little, finding it interesting that he was not able to give it away or ignore the urge to eat it, even when I had asked him to. My little outside force encouraging him not to eat it was no match against the inside forces and outside forces telling him that it was necessary, fine, and good to eat that dessert. It was too much for him to withstand.

The social eating structure in our environment is a powerful force that keeps us eating unhealthily. Have you been to a birthday celebration recently? What kinds of foods were served at this celebration? How about a wedding? A graduation? Holidays? When people around here get together to celebrate, they serve a lot of foods filled with overt and covert sugars, cooked in unhealthy oils, and refined to taste as fabulous as can be.

Fast forward to another example of a catered lunch at BYU in 2014. This time I was one hundred percent off all covert and overt sugars and refined grains. Excited does not describe my emotion this time. Walking into this lunch, I was scared that I had paid ten dollars for a meal I wouldn't be able to eat. I sat down. A dessert sat above the dinner plate, strike one. A small plate of plain greens was before me, and people passed around a poppy seed dressing for it, strike two. I ate my greens and watched as people passed around the white rolls, strike three. A server brought around a tumbler full of sparkling apple cider, strike four.

I drank my water and waited, sweat dripping down my forehead. *What would the main course be?* It was chicken and pasta covered with a sweet glaze. Strike five. I pushed aside the pasta and glaze and ate the chicken, trying to communicate to my friend next to me why I was acting like an anorexic, paranoid, health nut. She ate her cake happily and I continued to sweat and feel uncomfortable that in my attempts to explain myself, I was telling her what she was eating was basically poison. It was an uncomfortable situation and one that had me seriously questioning my resolve to fight food evils.

The only social taboo that seems to be in place at this time regarding eating healthy is the intolerance of weight gain. When I see people resolve to eat healthy, I rejoice. When they post before and after pictures of themselves to keep them motivated to eat right and keep the weight off, my heart sinks. Outward appearance is a socially judgmental reason to eat healthy. It's based on judging others or self as inferior due to added weight.

If that's what motivates you then it's a great start, but let me caution you that it won't last. It's wonderful to want to look your best if you keep in mind that looking nice is a motivation that can only go so far. Psychological and biological forces, combined with living in a land of plenty and no one but yourself to restrain you, will kick the "great body" motivation out from under you fast. It is not a strong foundation. It is based on an All or Nothing cognitive distortion that "I'm only valuable if I look great," which couldn't be farther from the truth. You are valuable just as you are, right now, whatever your looks, weight, or age.

Rituals, Traditions, Family Expectations

When I first attempted to go off sugar, how to abstain and still have fun in social settings was one of the hardest parts of the deal. I have a lot of family. I'm the oldest of ten, and my husband is the 2nd youngest of eight, so there are a lot of birthdays, a lot of get-togethers, and a lot of food! Every time food was served, if people saw me not eating they had to say something. It was interesting how quickly people noticed. I did not try to bring attention to it. I simply refrained.

My family members couldn't comprehend how anyone could stand by and not eat fudge jumbles, peanut butter fingers with fudge frosting, peanut butter cup ice cream, mint brownies, homemade chocolate chip cookies, iced cinnamon rolls, chocolate cake, s'mores, banana boats filled with chocolate and caramel, and on and on. "Can you just have a taste?" or "You don't even want one bite?" were asked of me so many times that I wish I had a dollar for every time I heard that. Family members had inadvertently become forces trying to pull me back to my old ways. It was difficult to explain, "No, I can't even have a bite, for that will set off in my system an uncontrollable cascade of biological and psychological forces that will make keeping healthy boundaries with food more difficult."

There is a general consensus in our social environment that over-consuming sugar is not only fine but expected at social events. There is no taboo yet on over taxing your system with unhealthy foods, especially if the point of the activity is to relax, live a little, and have fun. Since there are so many birthdays to celebrate, this is not just an occasional splurge.

I myself have served many things at social gatherings in the past I wouldn't eat now, so I don't wish to come across as judgmental. My intention is cautionary. These are forces you will contend with if you don't "go with the flow." Think about how you will compete against the forces of social expectation. There are so many different opinions of what "moderation" looks like, and so many misconceptions about what "healthy" is and is not, that it is nearly impossible at this time to come up with a balanced consensus.

My plea is that you hold to what you know to be right for you, based on what you have learned and what the Spirit has directed you to do. Personal integrity means that no matter how many people do it or say it's fine, you hold your ground. "Right is right, even if everyone is against it. Wrong is wrong, even if everyone is for it."[67] I may not have had all the right answers, but I was trying to hold to what truth I had been given.

Being Different but Part of the Tribe

Change can cause you to feel ostracized from the tribe at first. Being invited to a family gathering and bringing your own food to eat can cause you to feel odd or others to feel uncomfortable that

---

[67] Quote by William Penn

they are eating what is served. I have learned how to stand by my values without making a big deal about breaking the social norm. We still want to do our best to be part of the tribe.

But I didn't always know the best way to go about this. The first birthday I tried to celebrate for my daughter that was sugar/junk-food-free was a nightmare! My daughter was so distraught that her friends would have "no food" that my husband basically took over, and I cried in my room as I listened to children eat corrupt foods we were providing them. I've been to wedding receptions and come home emotionally drained after watching everyone else enjoy the refreshments. I admit I've even stayed home to avoid that feeling.

Just as I learned to overcome physical and emotional withdrawals, I learned to overcome feeling self conscious or bitter. "Never make a problem to be solved more important than a person to be loved."[68] I attend family events and love those there instead of worrying about being uncomfortable and staying home. I learned to make my own whole food, organic, and naturally sweetened treats to serve at birthdays. I'm trying to show love to my family and do the socially expected thing at a birthday party—serve something fun to eat.

Food Processing and Politics

In the last one hundred years, most especially the last fifty years, there have been some general movements in history that have spearheaded our move away from whole foods. The first was when the baby boomers were born after the world wars. There was a move away from whole foods to make foods that are easily stored, convenient to prepare, affordable, mass produced and palatable.[69] If we are going to feed millions of people we need to have a way to store food and mass-produce it! And sugar's a great preservative. Fiber does not store well, so the less fibrous and the more sugary the food, the better the storage life.

---

[68] Quote by Thomas S. Monson
[69] See "Fed Up" Movie Documentary

Another movement that may have contributed was the liberation of women. As the demand for equal work rights for women went up, the number of home-cooked meals went down, and the demand for convenient, quick meals became high. Let's face it, most women in the first half of the 20th century were homemakers, expected to keep the family fed.

I myself am a beneficiary of this movement. I am able to write this book in large part due to the fact that I was able to get a Master's degree while still a mother of three young children, something nearly unheard of a hundred years ago. I fed myself and my kids frozen waffles, freezer burritos, and corn dogs just to get through those years.

The third movement was a surge in the 1970's in the health organization and food industry that resulted in the eliminating of fatty foods in our diet.[70] So many adults were getting sick and having heart problems (specifically high cholesterol and weight gain), that doctors and experts called for reducing fat in the diet. When fat is removed from a food item, it tastes terrible, so sugar is added to make it palatable. High demand for low fat, good tasting food drove food companies to produce sugar-filled processed foods.

I am not saying any of these movements were wrong, many people the world over have been helped from having storable, convenient foods, more women in the work place, and exercising caution on eating high fat foods. I am saying that one side effect caused by these movements was a move away from whole foods.

Overconsumption of Convenience Foods

Food choices became driven by taste and time restraints, and today cooking and preparing food has become either a nuisance or a specialty; no one has time, let alone interest, to cook! But eat we must, so we've settled into a new way of eating. The new ways of eating are all about "fast," "grab and go," and we have microwaves

---

[70] Fed Up Documentary

that speed up the process even further (that some would argue heavily are also turning our food into a toxin).[71]

My substance abuse course professor informed the class that the average person one hundred years ago consumed about five pounds of sugar a year, and today the average person can consume about one-hundred and fifty pounds of sugar a year.[72] Instead of having homemade meals with occasional desserts, people now eat cheap, convenient foods made with processed added sugars with occasional vegetable sides.

Humans Tampering with Food

The last point is that humans are creating artificial foods to make food sweeter and more affordable and convenient. High fructose corn syrup is a manmade sugar, about the farthest thing you can get from a whole food. Scientists came up with a way to refine corn syrup so that it is even sweeter than it is, and thus changed the molecular structure in the process, making a cheap variation that is highly potent.[73] This is added to many foods you would not expect, like meats, and is a number one ingredient in processed drinks like soda and juices. High fructose corn syrup is to corn what cocaine is to a cocoa leaf or powdered sugar is to the sugar cane.

Then there are the artificial sweeteners that don't have anything to do with real sugar. Be sure not to replace sugar with artificial sweeteners, which I will label as bad or worse. The bad guys include aspartame, saccharine, neotame, sucralose, acesulfame, and cyclamates (i.e. Nutrasweet). They all break down into deadly acids in the body.[74]

---

[71] Leslie Korn, pHD Behavioral Medicine. "Nutrition and Mental Health" lecture, www.drlesliekorn.com

[72] Amy Pollard quoting The United States Department of Agriculture statistic: The average American eats between 150 and 170 pounds of refined sugars a year.

[73] See wikipedia "high fructose corn syrup" and "The Bitter Truth" lecture by Robert Lustig for more information

[74] On artificial sweeteners, see Robert and Shelly Young. *The pH Miracle*

Think of how un-whole food has become. If you eat an apple, you get some fructose, but you also get a lot of fiber, live enzymes, and vitamins to help process it slowly and efficiently in your system. Even sugar cane is rich in B vitamins and fiber, but white sugar is straight sucrose with no nutrient value that moves fast into the blood stream. Cocoa leaves were chewed for medicinal purposes for centuries, but you refine it into powder and it's one of the most harmful addictive substances made.[75]

Take tomatoes and ketchup for example. Tomatoes are rich in vitamins and minerals, have a good pH level for your body, are full of water and fiber to aide in digestion, and have some fructose in them to make them desirable to eat. Ketchup is a tomato that has been peeled, crushed, juiced, pasted, canned, filled with preservatives and added color, and combined with a man made sugar high fructose corn syrup. In essence, the tomato has been refined to a highly concentrated, high sugar carbohydrate that will wreak havoc on insulin and leptin. Ketchup will store well for years, and it tastes better than tomatoes. Unfortunately ketchup is no longer a whole food.

Land of Plenty

We have plenty of food in the United States in quantity and variety. If we lived on an island where the only food raised and harvested were crabs, fish, coconuts, vegetables, and maybe some honey or rice, in addition to individual vegetable gardens and fruit trees, we would not have nearly the amount of food insults as we do here. Or if we lived in a time when we only could eat what food was in season as the Word of Wisdom suggests, we would only eat food when our bodies needed it. Think about the difference; food would be fuel and there would possibly be few (if any) overweight people at all.

---

[75] Leslie Korn, pHD Behavioral Medicine. "Nutrition and Mental Health" lecture, www.drlesliekorn.com

But would that be a good thing or a bad thing? There may also be very little joy in eating, possibly undernourished people, and the plague of hunger. During times of scarcity, food must be rationed in many countries in the world. Even today there is much want and hunger in some countries, but in those areas there are no problems with over-eating and over-consuming sugar! Is it a good thing or a bad thing?

We live in a land of plenty, which comes with a lot of benefits, but the risk is that we could become like the people in *Cloudy with a Chance of Meatballs.* Their lives were so bleak and miserable when they only had sardines to eat, and then (thanks to a technological invention) they had whatever food their hearts desired without working for it, and what joy! But the only person showing restraint or concern about it was the old man who worried that playing outside the laws of nature might get out of control. He asks Flint, "Can you look me in the eye and promise me this will not get out of control?" The cartoon people went from one extreme to another. Both have consequences. Now that we have so many wonderful options of food at our fingertips, how are we ensuring that it won't get out of control?

Technological Advances

In the production of food, thousands of years of farming knowledge has been lost from individual families. In *Foodwise,* author Wendy E. Cook points out how our land of plenty and technological advances in farming have alienated us from nature and the way food should be grown and eaten. She says:

> I see great machines programmed by computer distribute fertilizers and pesticides in a vast landscape, a monoculture of wheat. There are no people, no weeds, no trees, no birds and no insects. And I imagine the great and sad voice of God, of a designing intelligence, saying, 'What have you done with the garden with which I entrusted you?'

Cook further states, "Bio-technology professes as its motive the solving of world hunger but in fact seeks to monopolize and exploit seed culture and destroy the wonderful genetic diversity created over millennia by small famers. Meanwhile, millions of Westerners suffer from diet-related illnesses."[76] Observing that there are products on our plates that are mildly poisonous, consciousness altering, addictive and deleterious to health, she calls for more people to bring back the old ways of eating or risk unknown consequences of changing our chemistry as we have changed the chemistry of the food we eat.

Overeating/Food Addiction

Outside forces often kick-start over-eating problems and food addictions, and these quickly become inner forces that are difficult to contend with. You can cause problems even eating healthy food if you are eating too much of it. Obesity and food-related illnesses existed even before man started altering food.

When I eat too much I have nearly as many problems with digestion as I do when I eat refined food and sugar. There is only so much storage space for glucose, only so much stomach acid to handle the content, and only so many enzymes and insulin to manage the digestion. Yet it is very tempting in a land of plenty to eat for eating's sake and minimize the consequences of throwing caution to the wind.

Eating Disorders

Eating disorders can become an unintended consequence of being too cautious. We don't want to think (or have our children thinking) we can *never* have sweet food, manmade food, or fattening food, otherwise they will be paranoid and anxious about eating

---

[76] Cook, W. *Foodwise: Understanding What We Eat and How it Affects Us, The Story of Human Nutrition*. Kindle edition, loc 291. Clairview Books, 2003.

anything! I have had young clients with peanut allergies afraid to eat anything because of potential contamination. I have observed children as young as eight years old refusing to eat because they were bullied about being chubby, despite what their parents do to convince them they are beautiful, that everyone is different, or not to worry about what others say or think. Unfortunately, the exaggerated danger of eating in their mind trump the parents' opinion, and the child still feels food is the enemy.

This is a difficult balance to strike. When I see a child in need of diet intervention, I struggle over how to teach them to limit certain foods without making them afraid to eat. Controlling eating too much puts our body into starvation mode, which causes other health problems. Children tend to see things in black and white, so it's hard to explain why it's not "bad" but rather unhelpful, and it makes things worse to develop anxiety over it.

Adults are not immune to this. I have observed, and experienced, the issue of trying to get too healthy or too pure in eating. This is a new extreme called Orthorexia Nervosa. The National Eating Disorders association describes the phenomena as follows:

> Those who have an "unhealthy obsession" with otherwise healthy eating may be suffering from "orthorexia nervosa," a term which literally means "fixation on righteous eating." Orthorexia starts out as an innocent attempt to eat more healthfully, but orthorexics become fixated on food quality and purity. They become consumed with what and how much to eat, and how to deal with "slip-ups." An ironclad will is needed to maintain this rigid eating style. Eventually food choices become so restrictive, in both variety and calories, that health suffers – an ironic twist for a person so completely dedicated to healthy eating. Eventually, the obsession with healthy eating can crowd out other activities and interests, impair relationships, and become physically

dangerous. Signs are 1) it is taking up an inordinate amount of time and attention in your life; 2) deviating from that diet is met with guilt and self-loathing; and/or 3) diet is used to avoid life issues and leaves you separate and alone.[77]

I have observed this in one client, a man who I will call Matt. Matt started a health food company twenty years ago, and it became so popular he became very stressed and overworked. Due to mounting physical and mental health issues he had to quit. He was so consumed about what he ate it was actually causing his health problems. He spent his whole life buying organic, healthy food, preparing, and cleaning up food. He was anxious, had viruses, weighed only ninety-five pounds, was alone at fifty-five years of age, and unhappy. That is orthorexia at its most vicious. Matt caused more problems than he solved stressing so much about religious eating.

I myself fell prey to orthorexia the year I started to become aware of food evils. I let my life revolve around what I was eating and spent exorbitant amounts of time and money on food. Unfortunately, I also felt a moral superiority to those around me because they didn't "know better" to eat whole food. I nearly let my identity become wrapped up in how I looked too. It was a slippery slope that I was able to climb off before it got really bad. Thankfully The Lord corrected me and I listened to His correction.

Antidote to Extremes

Dallin H. Oaks once spoke about letting your strengths become your weaknesses,[78] and I attended a lesson on this talk. I was squirming in my seat the whole time because I knew it was meant for me. I had let a strength of being more wise about what I eat become a weakness. Satan was using this weakness to destroy my

---

[77] http://www.nationaleatingdisorders.org/orthorexia-nervosa
[78] October 1994 Ensign, https://www.lds.org/ensign/1994/10/our-strengths-can-become-our-downfall?lang=eng

relationships and cause me more stress and anxiety. I didn't like realizing I was wrong, but I knew I could turn it into a learning experience instead of a thorn.

I corrected my course after that day, no longer focusing only on one virtue, to the annoyance of everyone around me, and creating more pain and difficulty for myself. I stopped writing on my blog, I stopped writing my "Thirty-day clean out," stopped caring so much about if I "slipped up," and started to just eat whatever the situation and social forces called for. And that was right before my horrible painful experience in Jerusalem. Another learning experience: I'd let myself slide back too far!

I learned again what I eat definitely affects how I feel and what my body can do, but I became more humble, sought medical help, and resolved to say, "I accept God's will for my life and my body." That's when I was led to knowledge about my unique metabolic needs. Instead of being a know-it-all with determination to eat pure, my mission focused on being wise about food choices, to realize that it will be a bit of a fight in our current food culture, and do what I can without going overboard.

Outside Force: Satan

Another force that is always there and always striving to influence our decisions is Satan. He too is often hard to detect. He can be crafty, or can outright manipulate our emotions, either way knowing our individual weaknesses and uses lies and deceit to make sure we are as miserable as possible. Although he does not create the emotions our brains and bodies generate, he can utilize them to his advantage with negative thoughts and sensations that create even more negative anxious emotions.

I started out calling this program a nine-step FOODFIGHT. But as I was writing the last chapter I realized FIGHT is not the word I want. Fighting only perpetuates the cycle that keeps us stuck. The more we feel pain, bad, overwhelmed or stressed, the easier it is for

Satan to get in there and utilize his deceits that cause us to feel depressed and afraid. We are then driven to eating unhealthy foods that give us relief.

That may lead to feeling shame or sadness, and that's when Satan jumps on the opportunity to fuel your brain with cognitive distortions that create fear. The chemical response of the body to fear will generate biological responses such as panic symptoms, fatigue, heaviness, pain disorders, and even painful digestive responses. So it does no good to try and "fight." Acceptance of whatever emotion we are feeling and training our brain to think in truthful and rational ways when you experience an emotion lessens the influence of Satan.

Marc David advises us that when we say or even think, "Don't eat that food, it is bad for you," what people and ourselves hear is, "You are a bad person for eating that food." To have someone judge our choice of food or simply believe they are judging us is the seedbed for negative emotions. "Consuming 'bad' food has never turned anyone into a bad person nor has eating 'good' food made anyone a saint."[79] I changed the name of the program to FOODLOVE because true love does not judge, true love does not abuse, true love thinks of the needs of others. To have a healthy relationship with food we need to bring the love in, and the outside force of the adversary is then abated.

Spiritual Principle 3: Faith

It takes faith to move forward because sometimes things get worse before they get better. Please trust me that things will be better in the long run! I also ask you to have faith that inside and outside forces are not stronger than God; we can overcome any weakness and any opposition with His help. Have faith that you are on the right track and you do not need to fear.

---

[79] Marc David *Nourishing Wisdom*

Have faith that you can do hard things. The body is a temple. With so many food corruptions coming at us with little in our control to stop it, we must be wise about what we consume, even though it is hard. We want to be as disease and pain free as possible because keeping our bodies and minds clean and pure is part of battling the adversary. God has commanded us to "bridle all our passions."[80] In doing so we will be filled with love and clothed with the armor of God. Again, this will be hard.

Keeping the temple of your spirit clean will be a shield, just as faith is a shield, against the adversary. Take the shield of faith with you as you move through the FOODLOVE program. Paul exhorted us to "Put on the whole armour of God, that ye may be able to stand against the wiles of the devil. Stand therefore having your loins girt about with truth, and having on the breastplate of righteousness, and your feet shod with the preparation of the gospel peace, above all taking the shield of faith, wherewith ye shall be able to quench all the fiery darts of the wicked. And take the helmet of salvation and the sword of the Spirit, which is the word of God."[81]

Are you a victim of food corruptions or are you a warrior? Time to become a warrior! The Spirit will give you the knowledge you need to move forward. All light and truth comes from God, if we humbly seek the truth, He will enlighten our minds through the Spirit. Living worthy of the Spirit is striving valiantly each day to watch ourselves, our thoughts, our words, our deeds, and continue in faith[82] that we perish not. Then our bodies will become a worthy temple for our spirits to dwell.

Challenge 3: The Food Diary

Part of observing how food affects you is to discover what your metabolic needs are. Are you sugar sensitive? What is your historic

---

[80] The Book of Mormon, Alma 38:12
[81] The New Testament, Ephesians 6: 11-17
[82] The Book of Mormon, Mosiah 4:30

genetic makeup? Carbohydrates, meat eating, or vegetable eating? What foods do you dread going without? What foods do you most enjoy? Most despise? What bacterial strains are you feeding?

Start observing what you and those around you intake. Which food insult is bringing you the most misery? Every system is a little different. I am highly sugar sensitive because of my limited muscle mass, fast metabolism, and genetic predisposition to have issues with my pancreas and insulin regulation. What type are you? A fast oxidizer? Large muscle mass? Store fat and never lose it? Thin on the outside and fat on the inside? Problems with inflammation? Thyroid? Chronically constipated or have issues with diarrhea? In order to know what the best course of action is for your future diet, or way of life, you need to know how your body responds to certain insults. Measuring what you eat aides in improving nutrition.[83]

For the next seven to ten days, please keep a food diary, writing down what you eat, what your digestive response is, and how you feel throughout the day. Below is an example of a simple food diary, but you can make it as detailed as you would like. Keep in mind that not all mood states occur directly after eating, so any time you feel "off," even if you haven't eaten recently, write that mood in the food diary.

What I ate/time	Digestive Response	Mood/Energy level

[83] Pritcher, Ashton. *Health Bent: 50 Everyday Nutrition, Exercise, Medical, Mental...Habits to Improve Your Health*. Amazon Digital Services, 2015.

Chapter 4: Dare to Change

*Only the human being keeps omnipotentiality—the freedom to
develop or specialize in many ways.*

Wendy E. Cook

If you are still reading I'm guessing you are convinced that
changing your boundaries with food is important. In this step, you
start to make a change in your food habits. This is exciting! I'm so
glad you have kept with the program so far.

The Seven-Day One Meal Challenge

The first, small change in your food habits is to pick one meal
and eat only whole foods for that meal. Make this change for seven
days. You are allowed to eat what you are used to eating for all other
meals of the day, but for one meal make sure it is only whole
foods—no refined, processed foods or sugars of any kind.

My suggestion is that this meal be breakfast, and the reason why
is because most of the standard American diet corruptions are
generally found in traditional breakfasts. Our ability to digest heavy
proteins and extract vitamins and minerals is optimal in the morning
when your stomach acid is at its prime. I have also found that my
ability to eat food that doesn't taste amazing and my strength to
overcome cravings is greatest at the beginning of the day. (This is
assuming that you've had a good night's rest and are otherwise active
and moderately healthy. If you have severe health problems,
insomnia, or a severe mood disorder, please see a health
professional.) So consider making your first change a breakfast
change.

What do you usually eat for breakfast? I used to eat cereal or
toast or both, maybe with fruit on the side to make it more "healthy."
Sometimes it was frozen waffles or pancakes with manmade syrup.
Occasionally I would cook a high protein breakfast of bacon and
eggs, but it was coupled with toast, pancakes, or fried hash browns.

Some just skip breakfast altogether! Are any of the above scenarios something you do as well? According to chapter one and based on what many nutritionists suggest,[84] this is an unwise way to start one's day. Would you be willing for seven days to adjust your breakfast and see what happens?

Training the Brain

If you have ever trained for an intense athletic event like a marathon, triathlon, or a sports tournament, you know that it is not wise to just jump in on race day and try to push your body to run. You have to train for it. You start small, a mile or two at first, and gradually run longer and faster until you have the endurance built to run hours at a time. The same principle applies here. I do not suggest you try to just completely eliminate all food corruptions all at once. Make a small change and do it for a short time period to train your brain and body to manage the differences.

The changing-breakfast challenge is the first step in confronting inside and outside forces that compel you to eat certain foods. Whether it is good to eat cereal for breakfast or not, I'm asking you to switch it up so that you can start taking control back when it comes to food. You will not have to eat only protein and vegetables for breakfast every day for the rest of your life. I'm interested to see if you can be the master over your intake. Trust me for now. Try the suggestions in this chapter, and in step six you will be the one to decide what is best for your body for breakfast.

I advise you, if you haven't already, to start reading labels so you will know what you can and cannot eat during the whole food challenge for breakfast. A whole food is the way God and nature made it, and the way it was intended to be ingested.

---

[84] Kathleen DesMaisons *The Sugar Addicts Total Recovery Program,* Diane Sanfilippo, nutritionist. *21 Day Sugar Detox,* www.balancedbites.com, Weeks and Boumrar, Dr. Leslie Korn

The Behavioral Contract

A therapeutic behavioral tool that helps people change habits and retrain their brain is the behavioral contract. This is a signed agreement that helps hold you to your commitment. Here is an example of a behavioral contract you can use as a template for your breakfast challenge. You can adjust the terms as you see fit for your first change.

---

7 DAY WHOLE FOOD BREAKFAST CHALLENGE

I, _____, promise to only eat whole foods and to not eat any refined food or sugar for breakfast for the next seven days.
This includes not eating:
- High fructose corn syrup
- Cane and Beet sugar
- Honey and Maple Syrup
- Artificial sweeteners, "diet" sodas
- Refined flours
- Processed fruit, grains, or dairy

If I adhere to this contract, I will receive
_____.

Signed_____

Date_____

There are three elements that your behavioral contract must include.

1) Your name, the dates, and signature

2) The terms you agree to commit to

3) A reward for completing the contract

Reinforce yourself for doing what you commit to. This will further train your brain to do hard things in the future. The incentive does not include food. We want to get away from thinking about food as a reward or comfort. Instead, choose an outing with your spouse or a friend, or a new outfit/purchase you've been wanting for a while. An overnighter out of town is another good incentive. Reward your efforts to change, and you will reinforce the change process.

What Can I Eat?

While you are changing breakfast, you may have the question, "If I can't eat processed foods and sugars, grains or fruit, what *can* I eat?" This is a good question. You can eat anything you can make yourself, and don't add refined flour and sugar.

It probably sounds like you are still limited. Are you still asking, "No really, what can I eat?" You will learn as you cook your own food there are many options besides prepackaged quick meals, even simple options. Simple yes, but not easy.

Let me answer your question with a question. Have you ever made your own mayonnaise? How about pickled your own cucumbers? Do you own a wheat grinder? Ever considered owning chickens? If you answered no, that may be why you are wondering what to eat. How do I have Mexican food if I can't buy tortillas and chips and enchilada sauce? How do I grab a snack without granola bars and trail mix?

Convenience in the Past

Just as we want to get away from the idea that food is a reward, we also want to get closer to the idea that you must work to eat. We have been trained to believe that convenience is coupled with food which limits our options.

On my website, I give an example of a recipe, and I include three different "levels" of difficulty. Level one is as simple as you can make it, which includes store bought, large-company-made foods. Level two includes some from-scratch elements and some store bought elements. If you want to make the entire meal from scratch, that is level three difficulty! Can you make a commitment to level three for breakfast for seven days?

79

In the *21 Day Sugar Detox,* Diane Sanfilippo gives us a whole recipe book of foods for breakfast, lunch, dinner, snacks, sauces, dressings, seasonings, and condiments, that have no sugar added, contain no white flour or pasta of any kind, and taste quite good.[85] But you have to work for it. I was exhausted at the end of every day when I cooked a meal from scratch for breakfast, lunch, and dinner, and I felt reverence and awe for my female ancestors who made everything this way. But I also eliminated health problems, noticed my hair growing back, and my muscles strengthened. So the question is not "what can I eat?" but "how much time am I willing to give to restore health?" I'm asking you to take some time for your body, your brain, and your family. You can do it!

In the epilogue I give some tips for simplifying, so no need to feel overwhelmed here. For instance, a friend of mine makes tortillas and bread once a month or so and freezes extras for later. You can make homemade anything—enchilada sauce, cream of chicken soup, pesto—in triple batches and freeze them for later.

It's about going back to basics in how we think about food. Our "land of plenty" has bombarded us with an abundance of fast, easy, affordable, great tasting food that has some drawbacks. If you make your own food you can control some of the corruptions. Go ahead and have sweet food now and then, just make it yourself and use naturally occurring sugars! If you don't work for it, there will be consequences that may come in the form of obesity, disease, mental illness, and death. Time to try your hand at working to eat!

Suggestions for Your Change

In case you need a little more detailed direction, here is what I would suggest. For the next seven days, for *breakfast only,* eat your choice of lean meats, eggs, nuts, seeds, and any vegetable or herbs and spices you want. Do not eat any fruit, grain, dairy, soy, sugar, or

---

[85] Diane Sanfilippo, nutritionist. *21 Day Sugar Detox,* www.balancedbites.com

unhealthy fat (vegetable oil, soybean oil, canola oil, corn oil, peanut oil) for breakfast. Go ahead and eat your regular diet the rest of the day. Just tweak this one element of your diet and see how you do. Commit to record your digestive responses and mood in your food diary.

There is a recipe compilation on my website www.wisefoodmind.com. I'd suggest taking some time in the morning to try out some of those recipes for breakfast. Remember, these are *not* traditional breakfasts high in carbs; these are comprised of high protein and nutrient dense foods. Here are some suggestions based on foods most people already know how to make:

- Baked chicken tenders and green peas
- Hamburgers on lettuce and tomatoes
- Chicken salad
- Boiled eggs and spinach smoothies
- Eggs any style and green beans
- Sautéed onion and peppers in omelet
- Bacon, fried eggs and asparagus
- Scrambled eggs with bacon bits and grapefruit
- Chicken veggie soup
- Chili

Here are some suggestions you can try from the recipe compilation:

- Sweet Potato Hash
- Vegetable Minestrone
- Tomato Basil Soup
- Tomato Basil Egg Casserole
- Oven-fried Sweet Potatoes
- Mustard Glazed Chicken Thighs
- Lettuce Wraps
- Italian-stuffed Bell Peppers
- Chicken Bryan
- Lemon Tilapia

- Shrimp with Lemon
- Spinach Avocado Smoothie

There are thousands of recipes available for free online from numerous sources. If I don't have anything appealing to you, Google search your favorite proteins and veggies to see what recipe ideas come up. This will be a good exercise in learning the principle of "working to eat." Once you learn the theory behind cooking, you will be able to create your own recipes. You may find you like making your heavy meal at the beginning of the day and eating a little more simply in the evening when you are tired or juggling other activities. Keep in mind you may need to get up a little earlier, prepare, and cook more than you're used to in the mornings.

Here is an example from my website of a recipe with different levels of difficulty:

Level 1

Mexican Egg Burritos
8-10 eggs
12-15 corn tortillas
salsa
avocado
butter or coconut oil
salt and pepper
turkey bacon (optional)
Prepare the bacon and chop into small pieces. Whisk eggs and salt and pepper together in a small bowl. In large skillet, melt the butter/coconut oil and pour egg batter in over medium high heat. Scramble/stir fry eggs until done. Turn off heat but keep pan on burner and add 1/2 cup salsa and the bacon to the eggs. Stir and heat through. Serve with corn tortillas, and avocado if desired.

Level 2: Make your own salsa

Restaurant Style Salsa
3 large tomatoes
½ red onion

2 jalapeno peppers
2 Serrano peppers
2 garlic cloves
1 -2 limes, juiced
½ bunch cilantro
1 tsp salt
2 8oz cans tomato sauce
Blend all ingredients except tomato sauce in blender until pureed.
Stir in tomato sauce until evenly red.

Level 3: Make your own corn tortillas

Corn Tortillas
2 cups Maseca Masa flour (made by soaking dry corn in lime water
and letting the outer shell of corn slough off, separating it out, and
allowing the inside meat of corn to dry again and grind into a flour)
1 tsp salt
2 TBSP oil
1 ¼ cup or more of hot water
Combine flour, salt, oil and water in a small mixing bowl. Mix with
your hands until you get a pie dough consistency, adding water or
flour to get it just right, not sticky but the dough holds together.
Cover dough with a wet paper towel to keep moist while making the
tortillas. Spread a piece of plastic wrap on counter and place a golf
ball sized dough ball on wrap. Cover with a second square of plastic
wrap, and press dough down with a glass pie dish or flat sauce pan
(or use a tortilla press if you have one). Press as thick or thin as you
want. You may have to flatten a few times. Immediately cook tortilla
in a skillet over medium heat, turning when the edges begin to lift.
Wrap in a cloth and keep warm in a tortilla warmer or covered pot.

Taking Responsibility

You are about to take the first step towards becoming truly
recovered from food corruptions. I hope it is exciting rather than
overwhelming. Many positive consequences come from working
hard for a good cause. You are beginning to operate under the

enlightened and true belief that our actions have consequences. Although it is important not to label food "good" or "bad" or people who eat food "good" or "bad" or anything like it, it is important to recognize that making a positive change where you can will have a positive consequence.

Marc David pointed out that many people want no rules or restrictions with diet and believe "anything goes" with eating. This is operating under the belief that no relationship exists between cause and effect. As if they are thinking *somehow, as long as I'm ignorant of the effect, whatever I eat will not have future consequences.* David suggests that they secretly fear responsibility, therefore they act as if responsibility were unnecessary.[86] I might have gotten a little out of hand the first year I started changing my eating lifestyle, but I was certainly trying to take responsibility for my eating habits.

What You Give

I know it is not easy, but you are not alone! Others are trying to take responsibility as well. Here is a transcript from a mother (and all these people are different! I'm not just quoting the same person) who talks about how she tried to change breakfast and some of the obstacles she faced.

> I don't know how it happened, but somewhere along the line I fell into the habit of giving my kids the rotation of Eggo waffles, instant oatmeal or hot cereal (Malt-o-Meal) laden with spoonfuls of sugar. Mom of the year here, right?(My kids would say yes!, the health experts would shun me I'm sure.) It's something the kids will actually eat, I didn't want them to go to school starving, and it's so easy and convenient for me.
>
> I've known for years that these aren't great breakfast choices, but I just didn't want to fight the battle. Well, I watched Fed Up a few weeks ago, and we decided we needed to do better

---

[86] Marc David *Nourishing Wisdom*

with the way we eat. Much better. I'm reading books, I'm checking out blogs, I'm talking to my friends who cut out sugar. Let me tell you, this is hard! I keep questioning myself. I'm grumpy and feeling guilty for putting my kids through this, except why am I feeling guilty over striving to give healthier breakfasts and food? This is my summer challenge. I'm not racing to take kids to school, so I have time to make better breakfasts and homemade snacks, but the disappointment and complaining is wearing on me and I'm second-guessing everything. It's been a week and I feel like crying.[87]

Why am I asking you to do something so difficult that will make you and your kids cry as you adjust? Why do hard things? I know in sharing the above I am running the risk of discouraging rather than encouraging you to change your eating habits, but I want to be honest with you. This is tough, but in the words of Tom Hanks, "It's supposed to be hard; if it wasn't hard everybody would do it. It's *the hard* that makes it great."[88] Furthermore, if you choose to take the more difficult road, I want you to know you are not alone and others have been there and conquered and come out smiling.

Wisdom You Gain

There is much wisdom to gain from doing something hard for a good reason. As I started to transform my diet lifestyle in order to fight the standard American diet, I struggled under the weight of the task. I realized that there was something biologically wrong with me that I am so sensitive to sugar, refined foods, unhealthy oils, hormones, artificial additives, and gluten. I am like the ultra unhealthy food barometer: if it's even slightly not healthful, my system reacts. My husband pointed out an analogy. I'm like a high-end, classy car and I need just the right maintenance or I break down.

---

[87] Quote used with permission, wishes to remain anonymous
[88] Quote taken from 1992 movie *A League of Their Own*

He is like a Ford truck that doesn't need as much fine tuning.

I can see that my fellow human beings are generally not as fragile, and can handle a lot more than I can without adverse side effects. For a time, I felt sorry for myself that I had to work so hard to maintain optimal health. I thought to myself, "I haven't got all the answers, solutions are not clear cut when it comes to food, and I am just one small weak person fighting an entire culture of ideas about food." However, I learned there was more to gain than health. Experience!

When I first learned there were food corruptions and consequences to eating sugar, I had a desire and to share what I learned and help everyone around me understand what they were doing to their health. I wrote on a blog nearly every day and tried to bring the subject up with people at church and in my family to let the world know this important information. I shoved my light in people's faces. People ignored it, or got intentionally vocal and pushed back. I had to learn that wasn't the way to help people.

Blog entry August 2014:

I feel as though I am letting my determination to "let everyone know about food dangers and never touch a single dose of toxic food again" cause damage to my relationships with family members, cause bitterness towards people making these foods available, and cause me to lose focus on other worthy goals. It is important to me that everyone in the world know what I have learned, I wish I could help more, promote awareness more, inspire more, but I want to love others more than I want to help them (and risk judging them), so I wait. Maybe God has an opportunity for me to fight this cause in an arena other than my own life someday.

I might not have all the answers, and solutions may not be clear-cut, but here is what I do know and what I have gained:

1. Some people are weak and need to watch what they eat. Some people are strong and don't need to be as selective, and God loves and accepts them both.

2. God is proud of me for recognizing my weakness and choosing to be very careful about my food choices and preserve this body he has given me.

3. There is no one right diet for everyone, because all metabolic types differ within in a culture, a community, and even an immediate family.

4. Sugar and refined processed foods that act as sugar are addictive and cause blood sugar dysregulation and imbalance to the digestive, circulatory, and hormonal systems in the body when ingested in high amounts on a regular basis in any human body.

5. No matter how important the cause or how great the truth, if our desire to help becomes judgmental, we aren't helping.

A healthy body we keep for this life; the above truths are life lessons that, when learned, we keep forever. That is worth the hard.

Love You Gain

Healing is more than *what to eat* and *what not to eat*; that is an old paradigm. It's about finding out why we are turning to food to fill the void. I learned a lot more than how to cook, and gained more than better health, from the determination to maintain healthy boundaries with food. I learned how to truly love myself through nourishing myself, and truly love food that nourishes, thereby not seeing my boundaries as deprivation.

Sometimes it is less about what we eat and more about the things we are dealing with in life that cause us to suffer digestively. What is your relationship with food? What is missing in your life, or is painful or stressful, that you crave pleasurable experiences through eating so often? You may have to address other voids in life like work fulfillment, relationship distress, unprocessed trauma, or not being who you know you were meant to be in life.

After one particularly grueling day editing this book, realizing how many mistakes I've made, and feeling like a fool for thinking I could write a book, my daughter came home from school crying because she had tried out for the school play and failed. We both felt miserable that evening, and the healthy vegetable soup I made was not nearly comforting enough. We started making jokes about how hard it was to choke it down, and soon we were laughing about other funny things until our sides were splitting. Believe me, we wanted the donuts and ice cream that night! Instead, we filled each other with comfort without using food.

God comforted us as well. He sent us a message that very afternoon through scriptures that our attempts to share our talents count, and He is pleased. The next morning I read Psalms 119:102-103, "I have not departed from thy judgments: for thou has taught me. How sweet are thy words unto my taste! yea, sweeter than honey to my mouth!" Love for my family and the love of God filled my void.

Chicken soup may not give us a physical happy feeling like you get from a surge of sugar, but at least it contains love. "Have you noticed how food that is 'offered' by someone tastes different from food you prepare for yourself? For me, even a cucumber tastes different if someone else cuts, peels, and serves it with love. Just as food absorbs the flavor of spices, it absorbs the attitudes of those who cook and serve it."[89]

It's about love. Every time I cut my kids' grapefruits or prepare a salad for my husband, or make myself a meal, I notice the love I'm putting into the food. That is a tangible ingredient that if received will fill not only our bodies but also our spirits.

---

[89] Marc David *Nourishing Wisdom*

Blog entry August 2014:

This school year I am making my kids lunches. I get up at 6:00 am so I can make a healthy breakfast and then pack three healthy lunches before 7:30. Working out must come later because morning is my food preparation time to keep myself and my children free of the Standard American Diet food corruptions.

I still keep our pantry clear of sugary refined foods and cook from scratch. I still make dinner and rarely go out to eat. I still read food labels. This next month is emergency preparedness month, so I plan to stock my food storage with foods I can tolerate (which limits my options quite a bit because the refined sugary foods are what store well). I am currently writing a book that tries to simply explain blood sugar regulation so that young people can understand it, and my sister is illustrating it for me. I am making meals ahead in the freezer for my kids when I leave for my anniversary trip in October. I do it because I love my family and I choose to love my life as well.

Are you willing to try something new to give yourself an opportunity to "break up" with your old food habits and engage with a new way of eating? By doing so you may be forced to confront certain voids and fill them in other ways, becoming better in more ways than just healthful eating. Bring the love back into eating!

Spiritual Principle 4: Fasting

You can claim blessings from fasting. I know that fasting from excess sugars and inflammatory foods is different than a fast from all food and water, preceded with prayer, and done with a purpose. That is a glorious eternal truth and commandment given us from The Lord. However, I have noticed that in fasting from unhealthy foods (coupled with prayer and done with purpose), I have been blessed in many ways similar to blessings received when fasting on Fast

Sundays. As you read in Isaiah about the principle of the fast, see if you can find the parallels between traditional fasting and fasting from food insults of our day.

> Is not this the fast that I have chosen? to loose the bands of wickedness, to undo the heavy burdens, and to let the oppressed go free, and that ye break every yoke?
> Is it not to deal thy bread to the hungry, and that thou bring the poor that are cast out to thy house? when thou seest the naked, that thou cover him; and that thou hide not thyself from thine own flesh?
> Then shall thy light break forth as the morning, and thine health shall spring forth speedily; and thy righteousness shall go before thee; the glory of the Lord shall be thy rearward.
> Then shalt thou call, and the Lord shall answer; thou shalt cry, and he shall say, Here I am. If thou take away from the midst of thee the yoke, the putting forth of the finger, and speaking vanity;
> And if thou draw out thy soul to the hungry, and satisfy the afflicted soul; then shall thy light rise in obscurity, and thy darkness be as the noonday:
> And the Lord shall guide thee continually, and satisfy thy soul in drought, and make fat thy bones: and thou shalt be like a watered garden, and like a spring of water, whose waters fail not.[90]

Isaiah's words are beautiful and true! Being wise about food choices is a type of fasting— blessings come from fasting. Strengthening your spiritual resolve over bodily appetites gives you strength to overcome other weaknesses. As I and others have broken free of the yoke of food insults, I have witnessed heavy burdens undone, oppressed bodies being freed, hungry souls satisfied, and health springing forth. We are better able to serve others as we renew our own health and keep our bodies clean.

As we "hide not ourselves from our own flesh" and loose the

---

[90] The Old Testament, Isaiah 58: 6-11

bands of corruption in food, we have more light, more guidance, and we become like a spring of water that does not fail. When we serve healthy food, we are feeding the needy! When we stop pointing the finger of blame at politics and producers and stop telling ourselves that it's no big deal, but humbly do what we can to fight food insults, The Lord is with us, and we will be blessed. Maybe not immediately, but eventually, you will gain strength, health, and wisdom.

Isaiah 58:11 again: "Then shall thy light break forth as the morning, and thine health shall spring forth speedily: and thy righteousness shall go before thee; the glory of the Lord shall be thy rearward. Then shalt thou call, and the Lord shall answer; thou shalt cry, and he shall say, Here I am."

Challenge 4: Whole Foods For Breakfast

If you haven't started already, for the next seven days change your breakfast to only whole foods, cooked or raw. Eat as you usually do for the other meals and snacks throughout the day. Combine this step with the first three by researching what to cook, writing your mind chatter about food, and keeping a food diary. Keep the mindset "it is only for seven days" in the forefront of your mind. Any change you make is a step in retraining the brain.

For this challenge:

- Sign a behavioral contract, including start and end date, and reward for completion.
- Write what your digestive response is and your mood after breakfast, lunch, and dinner.
- Observe inside psychological forces that make this hard, or easier than expected.
- Write in your journal or on an ABC sheet what you learned or how you made this happen, i.e. thoughts that kept you going, schedule changes, mindset changes.
- Write down in your food diary what digestive responses and mood responses you get.
- Pray for strength and seek an accountability partner to keep you motivated.

Chapter 5: Loving Food and Life

Peace is the result of retraining your mind to process life as it is, rather than as you think it should be.

Wayne W. Dyer[91]

Positive Outcomes

How did the breakfast challenge go? It's going back to the old "eat like a king for breakfast, a queen for lunch, and a pauper for dinner"[92] mindset, isn't it? Did you have to start over a few times or did you make it happen the first week? What thoughts or behaviors kept you going? What thoughts made it more difficult?

Below is a transcription from another person I've coached during her "whole food breakfast" challenge.[93] I'm hoping your experience was similar to hers, because the positive effects outweighed the drawbacks even though it is difficult. Can you relate to this person?

> I've been feeling a lot better eating protein and veggies for breakfast. I've always wanted to eat better breakfasts. I've known for a long time how cereal is awful to eat, but I'm so lazy. I really need to just do it though. I finally finished researching. I love everything I've been learning. It is frustrating though that so much of these foods are everywhere in our culture! I'm doing good. It is difficult, especially when you are trained to eat carbs for breakfast, but it's going great. I feel much better in the mornings. We've made a couple of your recipes this week which has

---

[91] Quote by Wayne W. Dyer, in book *There is a Spiritual Solution to Every Problem*

[92] Wise adage heard from my grandmother Avonell Rappleye

[93] Used with permission, wishes to remain anonymous

been fun. I've lost eight pounds just by cleaning up some of my food. I can't wait to see what happens next!

In her experience, the thing that made it most difficult was that she had been "trained" to eat refined carbohydrates most of her life. But as she learned, researched, and realized that wasn't the best thing to do for her body, she became excited about retraining her brain.

Moreover, she felt much better and lost weight just by changing one meal a day for seven days. Just as I inadvertently lost weight when I stopped eating candy and sugar, her body did as well, indicating she was becoming clean.

Lazy vs. Learning a New Skill

She mentions that she considers herself "lazy," which I would like to address. When you have been trained to eat convenience foods, the dreaded thought of working to eat can make you feel like you are lazy. But you are not!

You do many hard things that you have been trained to do all your life, like getting up early to study and go to school. Perhaps you have not been raised on a farm and have less experience in preparing and harvesting food. However, if you are a typical LDS parent, you probably work hard every day for your family in many other ways: reading scriptures, shopping/errands, carpool, full and part time jobs, writing/blogging/recording family history, reading/social media, sewing/crafts/creating, organizing activities, serving in church callings, exercising, visiting and home teaching, and praying. Some of us also endure emotional pain, physical pain, or lack of sleep making it difficult to do it all.

You are not lazy. Maybe you aren't used to consistently working to eat. Now that you have learned what food corruptions are, the need to intervene, and how to combat the problems, you can train your brain to work at keeping your food healthful. It's less daunting when you're trained.

Ten Day All Whole Food Challenge

This chapter is designed to prepare you for a Ten Day Whole Food Challenge! For this, prepare to eat only whole foods and no sugar for ten days for all meals and snacks. You'll need to fill out another behavioral contract, and keep in mind that sometimes it gets worse before it gets better, so don't give up. Physical, emotional, and psychological withdrawals may occur. It means the body is cleaning itself.

Raising the Bar

If the breakfast challenge was a few miles on flat paved trails, then this challenge is ten miles with hills and rocky terrain. It is not the full marathon yet. We are still in training. And like my friend above, it is exciting to see what you can do and what will happen next!

This will require some time when you have few other commitments and will not be traveling. Look at your calendar and pick a realistic start date; for example, right during a move or when meeting a deadline at work may not be the best time to try and control your environment of eating. I would further advise you to take some time to clear out your pantry by giving away or locking away foods that will not be eaten for the next ten days.

Food Boundaries and Price Tag

One of my favorite speakers is Pam Stenzel, who traveled the country giving her motivational speech "Sex has a Price Tag." Her premise was not that sex was "bad" but that God created strict boundaries around sex for a reason. When sex was used outside those boundaries negative consequences happened. She was trying to promote awareness to young people to abstain from sex until they were married because she loved them. She did not want one more young woman with a sexually transmitted disease or unwanted pregnancy telling her, "Nobody told me." She wanted to spread the word that in the proper context, sex was wonderful, but outside that context it could become deadly.

I, too, wish to inform others of a price tag—a nutritional price tag. Glucose, saccharides, and fructose in the proper context (whole foods) are wonderful! Outside that context they can be deadly.[94] We are going to challenge ourselves to eat food in the way God intended it to be eaten. Love yourself enough to remove yourself from anything that you know isn't good for you.[95]

While in the process of writing this book, I was at a social event with some women I know and love one evening. We were playing a jeopardy game and the "game show host" would throw a piece of chocolate at us if we responded with the right answer. I answered a question correctly, and a chocolate candy came whizzing through the air towards me. I caught it and looked at it, and all the words I had just written earlier that day swirled in my mind. In my hand I held a small sample of refined, chemically altered sugar, refined cocoa, processed low fat and refined milk, most likely from a conventional dairy, and with no whole food ingredients. I didn't think it was "bad," just useless. In that form, this food had a price tag. I had a moment of realization. There was no feeling of secret desire, self incrimination, or pity. I saw that food for what it was and knew that I had raised the bar, not restricted or deprived myself. I was treating my body with more love and kindness by throwing it away.

Check Labels to Set Guidelines

There are many forms of sugar you want to be aware of so you can be sure to stay sugar free for ten days. Here are a list of names sugar goes by. After reading through them, let's do a food check of our own. It's time to be food wise!

Amasake, apple sugar, Barbados sugar, bark sugar, barley malt, barley malt syrup, beet sugar, brown rice syrup, cane

---

[94] John Yudkin and Robert Lustig *Pure, White, and Deadly*
[95] Quote by Robert Tew

juice, cane syrup, Carbitol, caramel coloring, caramel sugars, caramelized foods, concentrated fruit juice, corn sweetener, d-tagalose, date sugar, dextrin, dextrose, diglycerides, disaccharides, evaporated cane juice, Florida crystals, Fructo-oligosaccharides (FOS), fructose, fruit juice concentrate, galactose (Gal), glucose, glucitol, glucosamine, gluconolactone, glucose polymers, glucose syrup, glycerides, glycerin, glycerol, glycol, high fructose corn syrup, honey, Inversol, invert sugar, iso malt, Karo syrup, lactose, levulose, lite sugar, malt dextrin, malted barley, maltose, maltodextrin, maltodextrose, malts, mannitol, sorbitol, xylitol, maple syrup, malitol, mannose, microcrystaline, molasses, nectars, neotame, petose, polydextrose, polyglycerides, raisin juice, raisin syrup, ribose rice syrup, rice sugar, rice sweetener, rice syrup solids, saccharine, sorbitol, sorghum, sucanet, sucrose, sugar cane, cellulose, molasses, monoglycerides, monosaccharides, trisaccharides, unrefined sugar, xantham gum, zylos.[96]

Go to your pantry, grab whatever boxed food is sitting there, and read the ingredients list. Not the list of percentages of carbs, fats, and proteins, the actual list of ingredients. What were the ingredients in your food that indicate this is no longer a whole food?

In a Quaker Oats granola bar, right next to "whole grain oats" is "brown sugar," meaning there is about as much brown sugar in this as whole grain oats. Here is what the granola bar lists as the remaining ingredients:

- Crisp rice—not whole grain rice—refined rice flour
- Sugar
- Malted barley rice (not a whole food)
- Rolled wheat (gluten)
- Soybean oil (controversial as to whether it's healthful)

---

[96] Referenced in Kathleen Des Maison's book *Sugar Addicts Total Recovery Program*

- Sodium bicarbonate
- Soy lecithin (a mixture of phospholipids and oil derived from egg yolks, rapeseed, milk, and soy, itself not a whole food)
- Caramel color (food dye)
- Dried milk (refined)
- More sugar
- Chocolate liquor (a sugar)
- Corn syrup (we don't have enough sugar yet?)
- Processed rice
- Invert sugar
- Sugar
- Corn syrup solids
- Glycerin (sugar)
- Soybean oil (again)
- Molasses (sugar)
- Artificial flavors and preservatives

This food is not a true friend. It promises sustenance and instead takes away more than it gives. Love your body enough to set guidelines about such food. Start observing what you eat by reading labels.

Overconsumption of sugar is hard *not* to do if you eat processed foods. Go back to the ingredients label, and look at the nutrition information with the percentages next to them. How many grams of sugar does it say? In one granola bar the label says, "Seven grams of sugar" and "Seventeen grams of carbohydrates." Remember that any refined carbohydrate acts like sugar in your body, so basically you are getting twenty-four grams of refined sugars by eating one granola bar. One gram is equal to .203 teaspoons., or inversely one teaspoon is the equivalent of 4.9 grams. So twenty-seven grams of sugar is 5.478 teaspoons of sugar. The recommended daily allowance of sugar is six teaspoons (which of late has been debated as too high). You met your quota of sugar intake for the day by eating one granola bar.

Behavioral Contract Number Two

I strongly suggest you sign a behavioral contract again. Modify it to include the added restrictions: all whole food meals for ten days.

WHOLE FOODS ONLY CONTRACT

I commit to eating only whole foods and no sugars or refined foods for all meals/snacks for the next 10 days, starting on _____ and ending on _____. I commit to preparing the food myself, reading labels to detect covert sugars, and specifically avoiding the following ingredients:

- Beet/Cane Sugar
- Corn Syrup/High Fructose Corn Syrup
- Overt and covert sugars
- White/refined flour or grains of any kind

If I complete this commitment, I will earn

_____

Signed_____ Date_____

(Remember, it is only for ten days!) Give yourself a reward as incentive for completing the challenge, and make sure that reward is *not* food.

This challenge should give you an idea of the benefits of eating healthy in a personal way. You will be able to reintroduce natural sugars after the challenge, so don't worry. I'm not asking for a life of misery and non-sweet food. In fact, we address in chapter six why that would be unwise. I'm asking you to train your brain to start showing some restraint. Again it is important that part of preparing is to set a date for when this will happen, and sign a behavioral contract like the one shown here in order to keep you motivated to see it through.

What to Expect at Step Five

In my training as a therapist for addiction recovery, I learned the stages and types of withdrawals people experience who suffer from addictions.[97] Interestingly enough, I experienced these same stages as I eliminated refined sugar, grains, and other food corruptions from my diet. As you completely eliminate foods that cause addictions and imbalances in the body, you may experience some negative side effects. This is normal. The body changing means the body is healing.

People who are addicted to many different kinds of drugs can attest that withdrawal from any substance is difficult in physical, emotional, and psychological ways. However, once the brain and gut are trained to thrive not having that substance, the withdrawal symptoms die. Although you may still miss the experience, it is not as painful to be without your "drug of choice."

Physical Withdrawals

As your body cleans itself of stimulating substances, you may have some physical withdrawals such as headaches, shakes or tremors, feelings of weakness or fatigue, irritability, cravings, and mood swings. If you can reframe these symptoms as indications that the body is cleaning itself, it may help you to endure them. They generally do not last more than a week.

Cravings are a physical withdrawal symptom and thankfully do not last long unless you give in to them. If you have cravings, remember that you are starving unhealthy, overgrown bacteria in your micro biome that are signaling your brain for sugar, and you are taming dopamine. They are interested in feeding themselves, not helping your body. So resisting their call is a good thing. You can try drinking eight or more ounces of water every time you feel a craving coming on. One person told me that it helps her to think, "I can endure this craving for the next five minutes," because usually the craving subsides after two to five minutes.

---

[97] Substance Abuse course taught at Brigham Young University, taught by Amy Pollard employee of Division of Substance Abuse and Mental Health in Utah

When I first completely eliminated food corruptions in April 2014, I had physical withdrawals. There was a strange sensation when I tried to exercise that my legs would collapse. I had a few headaches, and I trembled a little the first few days. My body seemed to be screaming at me: *where are the carbs?* I remember going on a hike about a week into it and thinking I was going to die and I couldn't breathe. I would sit and rest more than I usually did when hiking, and I held on to a rock and said the words, "Hold the vision, trust the process," over and over in my mind until I finished that hike. I couldn't believe how weak I felt, and it didn't seem fair. After all, I was trying to help myself, not make things worse.

This was when I had to remember that sometimes things get worse before they get better. Our bodies can adapt! Eventually my physical body adjusted to the diet change, and I felt strong again.

Emotional Withdrawals

Emotional withdrawals, however, last a bit longer. These emotions occur because of the feelings you have long associated with food. If food is no longer eaten for pleasure, for comfort, or as a reward, negative emotions may come up. Anger, rage, sadness, feeling sorry for yourself, feelings that you are being deprived, or that it's just not worth it are all normal emotional side effects of changing food habits. Even anxiety and depression can be intensified as your body balances hormones and neurotransmitters in an effort to get to a better place.

My emotions were all over the place for the first few months. From righteous indignation to self pity, feeling forsaken by God to feeling especially blessed, feeling anger at my environment and culture to joy that I had so many options were all in the gamut of feelings I experienced. I remember feeling sad in 2012 that I would never have Junior Mints again, which seems silly to me now. Yet every time I gave up a food for good, I had to have a time of mourning. I went through a time of giving up all dairy and had the whole spectrum of emotions over that. White bread was probably the hardest food for me to give up. I would imagine myself burying that food in a grave and having a grieving time, along with the cakes, candies, and desserts I would never taste again.

I would have intense dreams of eating foods I used to enjoy, and often when I watched others eat I would have a happy emotion based on the memory alone of having once tasted that food. Those emotions are completely gone now. I don't even feel negative emotions when someone is eating something right in front of me and I can smell it. The emotions pass, and your body adapts to that as well.

Psychological Withdrawals

The longest withdrawal, which can last from three to eighteen months, is psychological. This is why building a strong foundation of knowledge about food corruptions is important, because the thoughts that are associated with food and how you were trained to eat will undermine even the noblest of intentions. I have tried to warn you of inside psychological forces from the get-go, but the only way to appreciate how powerful they are is to experience it for yourself. Perhaps you already have and that is why you are reading this book! If not, when you try to withdraw from food corruptions completely you will understand just how intense those forces are.

Triggers and thinking errors are psychological forces that keep you stuck. As you commence with your ten day challenge, notice when you feel the urge to stop. This is a psychological trigger and will take some response-prevention in order to combat it. Notice: what time of day are you triggered? What are your surroundings? What are you craving? What is your mind chatter? Please write down what you are thinking during triggers. It will help to recognize outside and inside forces that keep you psychologically stuck in unhealthful habits.

I asked one of my clients, who was struggling with

psychological forces keeping her addicted, to write down what she was thinking when she had doubts about overcoming her addiction. She wrote the words, "You say you will change but we both know what you are really like." After she wrote that down, she paused and looked at me. "Who's 'we'?" I asked her. She said it was Satan, and she was shocked she let him influence her that easily and amazed how easy it was to recognize his influence on her thoughts once she wrote down her mind chatter. You will feel psychological opposition. Sometimes when you are doing the best thing, the opposition intensifies. Write it down to see who the real enemy is!

Preparing to Prepare Food

As you prepare to ward off cravings and triggers, it's best to have some whole food, homemade snacks on hand. The week before your challenge, make in-between-meals snacks such as salted nuts, banana chips, beef jerky, kefir, or almond crackers. Create a meal plan for ten days with recipes attached so you have part of the battle of preparing food (coming up with the idea) already taken care of. Here is an example of a home-made, sugar free, recovered-sugar-addict meal plan, with recipes:[98]

Breakfast:

Tomato Basil Egg Casserole
10 turkey bacon strips
2 cloves fresh garlic, minced
2 TBSP fresh chives
10-12 eggs
10-15 fresh basil leaves
½ tsp salt and black pepper
1 cup chopped spinach
2 TBSP oil
1 cup diced tomatoes

---

[98] Recipes cited are either original or modified from a book or internet source for my personal preference. Feel free to alter any recipes for your personal preference.

Preheat oven to 375. Slice bacon into ¼ inch strips. Cook bacon in skillet and set aside. In a large mixing bowl, whisk the eggs, garlic, chives, basil, salt, and pepper until well combined. Stir in the spinach. Grease a 9x11 inch baking dish with oil, then pour the egg mixture into the pan. Top with bacon pieces and tomatoes. Bake for 30 minutes or until the eggs puff up and become golden brown on edges.

Snack:

Grain-free Nut Granola
2 cups whole or halved nuts of choice
1 cup slivered almonds
½ cup seeds of choice
½ cup almond flour
2 green tipped bananas pureed
1 egg
2 tsp vanilla powder
2 tsp cinnamon
½ tsp nutmeg
1/2 tsp salt
Preheat oven to 350. In a food processor, pulse the whole or halved nuts until they're partially ground and partially still in small chunks. Pour the nuts into a large mixing bowl, then stir in the slivered almonds, seeds, and almond flour. Place the bananas, egg, vanilla, cinnamon, nutmeg, and salt in the food processor and process about 20 seconds or until all ingredients are pureed. Pour the banana mixture into the nut mixture and stir until the nuts are well coated. Pour the mixture onto parchment paper lined baking sheet. Bake in oven for 30-35 minutes, checking every 10 minutes and turning the chunks of granola with a large spoon to break up large pieces. This allows it to dry out and lightly brown on all sides. Remove from the oven and let cool uncovered.

Lunch: (could be soup with homemade broth, or green salad with no dressing/homemade dressing/guacamole)

Spicy Chicken Soup
2 TBSP coconut oil or bacon fat
1 small onion, diced
red bell pepper, diced

2 carrots
2 celery stalks, diced
1 poblano pepper, optional
Salt and pepper to taste
2 tsp cumin
2 tsp ground coriander
½ tsp chipotle powder
7 ounces tomato paste
1 quart bone broth
½ pound boneless, skinless, chicken, cooked and shredded
Garnishes: cilantro leaves
1 avocado sliced
In a large soup pot, melt the coconut oil over medium heat. Put the
onion in the pot and cook until it becomes translucent and the edges
begin to brown. Add the bell pepper, carrots, celery, roasted poblano
pepper, salt and pepper. Add the cumin, coriander, and chipotle
powder and stir until well combined. Cook for a few more minutes
until the vegetables are soft. Stir in the tomato paste and bone broth
and season with salt and pepper again if needed. Reduce the heat and
simmer for 20 minutes or until the flavors are well combined. When
the soup is nearly done, add the cooked chicken to the pot just to heat
through. Taste once more and adjust the seasoning if needed. Serve
garnished with the cilantro and avocado slices, if desired.

Bone Broth
2 pounds meat bones, any kind
1 TBSP apple cider vinegar
4 quarts water
1 TBSP salt
1 clove garlic, smashed
Place all ingredients in a slow cooker and cook on high 1 hour and
low for 8 – 24 hours
Guacamole
4 avocados
juice of 2 limes
1 medium shallot, minced
¼ cup chopped fresh cilantro leaves
Salt and pepper to taste
½ jalapeno pepper, minced

Slice each avocado in half lengthwise around the pit, remove the pit, then scoop the flesh into a mixing bowl. Mash the avocado with a fork. Stir in the lime juice, add the shallot, cilantro, salt, and pepper and stir until well combined. If you like spicy guacamole, add the jalapeno and stir to combine. Serve chilled or at room temp.

Snack: (beef jerky, grapefruit, yogurt, apple, almonds)

Beef Jerky
1/3 cup cocoanut aminos
1 tsp granulated garlic
1 tsp onion powder
½ tsp sea salt
¼ tsp black pepper
1 pound lean beef
In a large bowl, whisk together the marinade ingredients. Taste it and adjust the seasonings as desired. It should taste stronger than you want the jerky to taste. Cutting against the grain of the meat, slice the meat in to approximately 1/8 inch slices using a very sharp knife or meat slicer. Place the sliced meat in the marinade and allow it to sit for up to 1 hour. Arrange the meat on trays in a food dehydrator and heat at 145 until the meat reaches desired dryness, 3-5 hours. In oven, set it to 200 degrees and bake for 2-4 hours until reaches desired level of dryness.

Dinner:

Pesto Spaghetti Squash
1 large spaghetti squash
Pesto:1 cup fresh basil
1 cup spinach
1/2 cup raw almonds or pine nuts
3/4 cup olive oil
3 cloves garlic
½ tsp real salt
¼ tsp pepper
1 TBSP sun dried tomatoes
Preheat oven to 400. Cut the spaghetti squash in half lengthwise and remove the seeds and inner membranes, then sprinkle liberally with salt and pepper. Place the squash halves face down on a baking sheet. Roast for 60 minutes or until skin gives when you press on it

and the noodles inside release easily from the skin. Meanwhile prepare pesto: Place all pesto ingredients in a blender and blend to a paste, scraping down sides if necessary. Add ½ cup parmesan cheese for a Parmesan Pesto variation. Taste for seasoning and add more salt, pepper, or basil if needed. While squash is warm, use a fork to remove the noodles, then toss with the pesto. Depending on the size of spaghetti squash you may have extra pesto.

Before bed: (Baked potato with skin on or plain oatmeal with blueberries)

Oatless Oatmeal
1/4 cup raw unsalted walnuts
1/4 cup raw unsalted almonds
2 TBSP ground flaxseed
1 tsp ground allspice
3 eggs
1/2 banana, mashed
1 TBSP almond butter
1 handful fresh berries
Combine the walnuts, almonds, flaxseed, and allspice in a food processor and blend to a coarse grain but not a powder. Set aside. Whisk together eggs and milk until thick like a custard. Blend the mashed banana and almond butter together and add it to the custard, mixing well. Stir in the coarse nut mixture. Warm the mixture in a saucepan over low heat, stirring frequently until the batter reaches the desired consistency. Top with berries and more milk if desired. Serves 2.

*   *   *   *   *   *   *

Simply delicious! Every recipe contains whole foods, some protein, some complex carbohydrates, lots of veggies, and there are hundreds more delicious, non-addictive, energizing and healthy recipes out there. We don't need excessive amounts of sugar to enjoy eating.

I created a ten-day meal plan for my ten day sugar free challenge. The formula was 1) lean protein for breakfast and lunch, carbohydrates in whole food form for dinner, and lots of vegetables, 2) no unhealthy oils or sugars or refined food. You can make any variation on the same formula if you desire, or whatever formula works best for you. All the recipes of my meal plan can be found on my website www.wisefoodmind.com under Recipes.

You Can Do It

What positive words did you tell yourself to get you through the seven day breakfast challenge? What benefits did you experience? Keep those thoughts at the forefront of your mind as you go whole food for ten days. It will go fast. Here is another transcription from a person who completed the challenge. This could be you too!

I did it! I went ten days without sugar! I feel so triumphant! The cravings weren't as bad as I thought they would be, I didn't starve like I thought I would, and I only got one nasty headache. I was really surprised actually at how I felt more full and satisfied by eating this way, and I had tons more energy! And I realized I don't need a sweet after dinner. The hardest part was preparing the food. It was hard to do it with a little baby. Also I noticed my milk supply has gone down during this challenge. My body has always struggled with milk production. But overall it was a good experience.[99]

I have been thinking a lot about my food journey. When I was a kid, I had no idea what was good food and what was bad. I just thought desserts were bad, had no idea about anything else. I thought a fast food kid's meal was pretty healthy! I was always taking too much rice at dinner and ate bread all the time. I feel I have come so far, especially these last few months. I'm so grateful for all I am learning. I want to help my children know about food and help them eat healthier. Thank you for helping me and for all the knowledge you have gained.

---

[99] Used with permission, wishes to remain anonymous

What a positive outcome from doing something hard! I was so grateful to be a part of helping this person experience immediate positive results from food fighting. I hope you experience this as well.

Spiritual Principle 5: Acceptance and Gratitude

As you prepare to reset your system and complete this challenge, you will be tempted to stress out over food and not enjoy what you can eat. This will undermine your efforts to burn calories, assimilate food, and gain the best nutrient from your food. There must be a measure of relaxation, presence, and gratitude when you eat in order for eating to benefit your body.[100] If you can embrace the gospel principle of gratitude, and trust that no matter how hard or painful this is God will help and heal you, you will save yourself from making this harder than it needs to be.

> Hear now my reasoning, and hearken to the pleadings of my lips. Will ye speak wickedly for God? and talk deceitfully for him?
> Will ye accept his person? will ye contend for God?
> Hold your peace, let me alone, that I may speak, and let come on me what will.
> Though he slay me, yet will I trust in him: but I will maintain mine own ways before him. Job 13:6-8,13, 15
> For I know that my redeemer liveth, and that he shall stand at the latter day upon the earth: And though after my skin worms destroy this body, yet in my flesh shall I see God. Job 19:25-26

These are the words that got Job through his difficulty. Gratitude will also offset the risk of it seeming like it's "not working" because the added stress of preparing food is undermining your efforts. Count your blessings during this stage. Thank Heavenly

---

[100] Pavel G. Somov. "360 Degrees of Mindful Eating: 5 Core Skill Sets to Overcome Overeating"

Father for the abundance of food we *can* eat, bless your food, and eat it slowly.

Acceptance of God's will and trusting His wisdom will help you heal. I was not able to recognize lasting change until I accepted the pains and embraced the work necessary to keep going. We don't know why we have to endure and work as hard as we do, but if we are going through it, there must be a reason because God loves His children. That is the way life is, and we must retrain our brains to process life as it is rather than how we think it should be in order to have peace.

Remember, some miracles take time. Change and refinement is not an instant process. Accept God's will for your life. Say to yourself every morning, "I accept God's will for my life and my body." Write down what you are grateful for on a blog or in your journal as I did below. Acceptance of God's will in combination with faith, knowledge, discipline, sacrifice, and deliberate efforts to fast from foods that might harm you, miracles can occur!

Blog Entry 12/1/14:

Today I am overflowing with gratitude for my life. I know I have entered old age kicking and screaming, so bitter and frustrated that my body doesn't function like it used to, but in many ways I still function very well. How fortunate I am! I don't spend nearly enough time writing about or thinking about how wonderful life is. I'm so busy surviving I don't take time to live.

I'm grateful for freedom to move and live according to my will, freedom from tyrannical government and freedom to worship as I choose, freedom to choose to be happy and friendly and kind to others instead of bitter and resentful. I'm grateful for companionship and love and family. I'm grateful for a smart, hard working husband who provides me financial security and trusts me with our finances. I'm grateful for three healthy intelligent children who are precious, learning, and doing their best with the life given them. I'm grateful for family and friends all around me, for those who listen and support and love me despite my weaknesses, who pray for me, and are there if I ever need anything. I'm grateful for cars, washers and dryers, dishwashers, phones, internet, and instant communication. I'm grateful for clean water, available and abundant food, and millions of recipes at our fingertips. I'm grateful for God, my Heavenly Father, and His Son, my Savior, and I trust him and will try to be patient, finding joy in each day and being willing to submit to His will no matter what.

"Oh, earth, you are too wonderful for anybody to realize you. Does anyone ever realize life while they live it...every, every minute?"[101]

Challenge 5: Ten Day Whole Food Challenge

- Start your Ten Day Food Challenge! Only whole foods and no sugar for ten days.
- Fill out the behavioral contract and keep in mind that sometimes it gets worse before it gets better, so don't give up.
- Physical, emotional, and psychological withdrawals may occur; it means the body is cleaning itself.
- Utilize the spiritual principles of acceptance and gratitude as you incorporate this change.
- Slow down, find pleasure in whatever you are eating, and think positively about yourself while you eat.
- Write down any positive changes.

---

[101] Quote taken from play *Our Town* by Thornton Wilder

Chapter 6: Optimal Diet Lifestyle

"Five key factors—life-style, environment, season, age, and health—interact to create a ceaselessly changing diet."

Marc David

Optimal vs. Perfect

You have come a long way if you have gotten this far. Learning what general food corruptions are and testing your ability to replace those corruptions with whole food prepares you for a life change. Let us take a break from changing food habits for a chapter to mentally gear up for the next step: tailoring an optimal diet lifestyle for you.

I would like to issue a caution right up front. We are *not* trying to find a "perfect" diet for you. A perfect diet does not exist. An optimal diet lifestyle is achievable—if you understand that an optimal diet is ever changing depending on the person, the place, the age, and the time, yet is ever steady in its standards.

Ponder these questions as we discover your optimal diet lifestyle. During the whole food challenge, how did you feel? After the challenge, what foods did you go back to? If you were to create a healthy eating regime for life, what would it look like? In this chapter we will explore the following to get a better perception of what "lifelong healthful eating" looks like for you. This includes:

1) What unique inside or outside opposition you might have faced.

2) How to refine the diet to make it optimal for you.

Unique Individual Forces of Opposition

As you decide to go healthy for good (chapter seven), there will be obstacles I cannot foresee because we are different. Withdrawals aside, you may experience some personal opposition unique to your situation and personality type. You may become too diligent about eating your ideal diet and obsessed or overly cautious about what you intake. You may become stressed about eating your ideal diet, see no results, and be tempted to give up. You may find it too tedious, too much work, too structured, too impossible to get right, too bothersome to those around you, or just not worth it.

Change is daunting and difficult for each of us in different ways. I can only attempt to share with you in more detail some of the difficulties I faced in hopes of preparing you for what lies ahead. Even though it may not be exactly like your experience will be, I believe it can help keep you moving forward.

Obsession

When I worked at the prison in the mental health department, we taught the female inmates about setting boundaries to prevent domestic violence. After these instructions, some women became too rigid in their boundaries as they learned how to train their brain to stand up for themselves, acting selfish and pushing people away. They had to learn to be vulnerable and nice after becoming obsessed with being assertive. In the same way, as I changed my food habits, my perception of eating clean was too rigid and extreme as I learned what my boundaries were. This eventually burned me out, and I had to regain balance.

Blog entry November 13, 2014:

The obsession of trying to figure out my problem and heal my gut has extinguished. I've made up my own lyrics for the song "Let it Go," and I sing it anytime I felt any kind of digestive discomfort. How do you like my version?

The things I've learned all haunt me tonight

No progress to be seen

A kingdom of confusion

And it looks like I'm the queen

The wind is howling like this swirling storm inside

Couldn't heal my gut, heaven knows I tried!
Don't eat sugar, don't eat dairy
Be the good girl you always have to be
Conceal, don't feel, and don't eat bread!
Or you'll be dead!

Let it go, let it go
Can't hold it back anymore
Let it go, let it go
Turn away and slam the fridge-door!
I don't care
If I waste away!
Let the storm rage on,
The pain never bothered me anyway!

It's funny how resistance
Makes effort seem futile
And the foods that once controlled me
Can't get to me at all!

It's time to see what I can do
To test my limits and break through
No right, no wrong, no rules for me...I'm free!

Let it go, let it go
I'm tired of asking why!
Let it go, let it go

You'll never see me cry!
Here I stand
And here I'll stay
Let the storm rage on!

My problems flurry in a dizzy guessing game
My doctors can't agree and speculate on what to name
And one thought crystallizes like an icy blast
I'm fine but not normal,
Obsessing's in the past!

Let it go, let it go
Who knows what's going on?
Let it go, let it go
That perfect girl is gone!
Here I stand
In the light of day
Let the storm rage on,
Pain never bothered me anyway! [102]

Experience can be a brutal teacher, I felt somewhat ashamed for taking it too far and adding stress to my life . You sometimes have to cross the boundary in order to find the boundary that works for you. Do not beat yourself up if you become a little obsessed at first in your attempt to reset your food environment. You will figure out what works for you. "Letting things go" helped me gain a more accurate perception of eating wisely.

---

[102] Original song "Let it Go" from Disney's animated film *Frozen*

114

Stress

Stress is counterproductive to the healing process. If you are rushed, overwhelmed, panicked, or overworked your body will create its own toxins (cortisol, the stress hormone, and adrenaline) that will keep you in a sympathetic state of arousal and make it difficult to rest and digest. When do you eat? Do you sit down? Do you chew your food so your stomach can get ready to produce the proper amounts of acid to get food to the right pH so your system triggers the appropriate enzymes? Do you think about what you are eating or what you need to do in the next five minutes? Is the body in a state where it can move things through in order or is it worked up and sporadically firing here and there throughout the digestive track?

However, it is frustrating when people tell you to stop stressing in order to reduce health problems, because it's not really possible. We have to stress a little. How does one stop caring about everything and still survive? Retraining the brain, changing how you think about things, as we discussed in chapters four and five, helps reframe stress from negative to positive and will provide a more accurate perception of eating wisely.

Blog entry January 7, 2015:

Fight and Flight or Rest and Digest? What if how we eat has more to do with digestion issues than what we eat? If you are eating on the run, gulping things down, thinking about the million things you need to do while eating, eating while working, not eating then stuffing yourself, scared to eat, hate to eat, etc, your millions of motor complexes and hormones, gut neurotransmitters, enzymes, and everything that goes with digestion are not going to be able to work efficiently.

We work very hard but not in the ways our ancestors worked—with their hands and their backs. We work with our minds. The stress we encounter every day puts strain on our system. Instead of being threatened once in a while by enemies, predators, or accidents that put a body's sympathetic nervous system on alert, we experience stress multiple times a day in smaller amounts that generate the same kind of response, which creates havoc on the digestion system. It's like death by a million cuts.

How can we get back to rest and digest in a modern world? A home cooked meal where we sit down and savor the food is a luxury. It's no wonder everyone is addicted to sugar—it produces the quickest pleasurable response. It's our modern way of enjoying eating.

I have a hard time with this. I'm by nature impatient and anxious, so getting myself in the proper "Zen mode" to eat is tricky. After a long week of stimulating my mind for work twenty hours, keeping track of kids' schedules and responsibilities, meeting my own schedule demands and responsibilities, trying to find the right balance between stress and rest is tricky. By Friday my mind is pretty worked up, sleep is difficult to maintain, and my stomach churns all night long. I have to take a day to rest, reset my adrenals, which helps my stomach feel much better, and then I sleep like a baby.

But if I don't stay vigilant, am I being slothful? We need to work to survive, and I live in a world where stress and work are usually yoked together—in my experience they certainly are. Can I break that yoke and work hard but not stress? Or what if stress isn't necessarily a bad thing? Is there a way to be stressed and be ok at the same time? I listened to a lecture by Dr. Kent today who has a word to say about stress and health:

"Stress is not always negative. The classic stress response is part of our general adaptation syndrome: when we feel a threat our body goes into defensive mode. Every living being

116

has a certain amount of adaptation vitality, energy and is designed to respond to stress. Non-living things are non-living because they don't have a nervous system with the ability to adapt; living beings can adapt.

"Complete absence of stress is not compatible with life. Saying "I want to eliminate stress in my life" is really a shame because the only time you are going to eliminate stress in your life is the day you die. If you are alive, you are adapting to stress and that's the essence of life and the human experience. Positive stress is what we seek as human beings—competing at an athletic event, falling in love, excelling in your life's purpose—those are all stressful, all require adaptation to change, but they bring exhilaration and growth. Why do people jump out of airplanes for a rush? Go to movies that make them cry? Stand up and sing in front of people? We want to expand the scope of the human experience."[103]

He goes on to say that cells can't be in defense and growth at the same time, and neither can people. The way to reframe stress from negative to positive is to change your perceptions or state of mind regarding something difficult. We need to somehow stop viewing life as a threat. We can change our perception about any part of it and allow our bodies to adapt and grow. Stress does not have to be "bad."

Misperceptions

It follows then that an accurate perception of what is going on in the world can offset stress that keeps us unable to adapt to change and stress. No wonder religion is so powerful in helping people endure life's difficulties! Having an eternal perspective can allow us to trust God and move forward. In the scriptures, how many times has God asked us to "fear not"? So many that I'm sure God believes we do not have any reason to fear if we are prepared.

---

[103] Christopher Kent, DC, JD. From his lecture "Stress: Good and Bad"

Therapy also helps people gain a healthy perception of life. Cognitive therapy assumes that it is not what happens to us, it is what we think about what happens that creates distress. This paradigm is helpful when we want to overcome negative emotions because it gives us a choice: change our thoughts. No matter what happens to us or what our mood is, we have a choice in how we think and behave.

I have attempted to give you a paradigm shift about food in this book. If you are trained to believe that eating the most convenient food possible is best and eating is just an annoyance that gets in the way of better things in life, you will struggle digestively. Not only because convenience food is unhealthy, you are not in "rest and digest" mode enough of the time.

Many of us have actually been trained to believe things that keep us stuck in eating food that isn't healthful. Maybe you have been trained to believe that food has to taste good to be worthy of eating, or that you have a right to eat food that is desirable and makes you happy, or that "junk" food really is not that bad. Maybe you have been trained to eat simple carbohydrates and sugar in the morning. After reading this book, what is a more accurate perception of food and eating?

The Medical Model

Then there is the medical model prevalent in our culture that suggests you can simply take medication to get rid of symptoms. Why go off sugar and gluten when I can just take an acid blocking drug to reduce symptoms of stomach acid imbalance? I'm not sure that blocking pain is the best way to adapt. What if a more accurate perception is to feel the pain and let your body tell you where an adjustment needs to be made so it can heal? Here is a viewpoint from a holistic health care professional trying to get away from the medical model:

> Pain killers may work, and that may be the worst possible thing that can happen. Telling your body to 'shut up now'

tells yourself there is no reason to pursue the cause of the pain. We have been mismanaged. Pictures tell the doctors this is where the pain is coming from, people obsess over structural problems, and take prescription painkillers. This tells the body to shut up which leads to other problems."[104]

I don't mean to suggest that painkillers or other medications don't have any purpose, but I'd encourage you to look at both sides. To assume it is good to block pain or be "pain free" at all times is a misperception. Doctors are only trying to help reduce suffering, which I applaud, but we need to be wise about listening to our pain and healing the whole body even if it takes a little work.

Misguided Advice

I've noticed when I see a person reaching out to people on social media about eating healthy, there are a host of responses from people who have "the answer." Others' transference of guilt, uneducated suggestions and advice, others' definition of "moderation" (depending on who we talk to and interact with) can all be unique outside forces that skew our perception of what our ideal diet should look like. Just as it is important to gather knowledge and learn, it is equally important to weed out the information that does not apply to us. We are all trying to figure this out and who knows yet if we are part of the cure or are we part of the disease?

I was guilty of being a know-it-all for a long time, ready to give a pat answer to what ailed people without considering differences in situation and temper. I came by it naturally (some of us are born a little more analytical than others). I still feel a desire to share information with others, yet now do so with caution. Even with the best intentions, those trying to help can actually harm instead, and I do not want to cause harm. Marc David issues the following profound caution:

---

[104] Dr. Steven Geanopulos, from lecture "Your Diagnosis: why labels can be dangerous and prevent you from seeing what else is happening" at *the Pain Relief Project*

119

Whenever you read diet books or listen to nutritional advice, remember you are probably receiving information from those who are reading their own bodies and translating it onto yours, presenting their philosophy of life through beliefs about diet, and proving their biases through scientific conclusions that can be interpreted in other ways.

Of course, we expect to find useful information when consulting expert sources, but the reality is that most authorities see only a small part of the nutritional spectrum, and no matter how much information we gather, we must inevitably make our own nutritional choices.[105]

Likewise, I may only see part of the nutritional spectrum and do not wish to confuse or provide a perception that is inaccurate. I have tried to present what I have learned in the most accurate and wise presentation possible; however, I am only human and limited in what I know. Therefore I urge you to glean from my words what you feel is true for you, and always consult with The Lord and follow the Spirit for what is best for you. With that caution, proceed to read how to refine your diet for life.

Refining Your Diet

Like All Others

In some ways we are like all others. In general, if a person over consumes food that is toxic to the body, it will start to break down at that individual's genetic weak link. For myself it was pancreas problems, depression, ulcers, and irritable bowel syndrome. For others, it may be cancer, MS, Parkinson's, thyroiditis, dementia, osteoporosis, allergies, or just a weak immune system. We can all take heed and practice wise food habits that will truly "nourish and strengthen" our body.

The food diary doesn't catch some of these things. For example, some people may feel fine after eating a lot of sugar all day, or some

---

[105] Excerpt from Marc David's book *Nourishing Wisdom*

people may feel sick eating breakfast in the morning. However, it is generally healthy to avoid overconsumption of sugar and to eat breakfast; your body's signals or lack of them may be misleading. Look to general guidelines about food related potential problems for ways we are like all others.

Like Some Others

Seeking information and medical help for your specific health issues is wise to learn ways to help your unique needs. I have a friend[106] who suffers from Hashimoto's thyroiditis[107] and has tried incorporating better foods and eliminating less helpful foods from her diet as part of overcoming the disease. She reads experiences and advice of people who have the same illness. Some of her research has been helpful for her. She has also sought appropriate medical treatment and advice, some which helps and some of which does not. Look to others with your same health challenges, to doctors, forums and support groups for ways you are like some others.

Like No Others

My friend noticed that even people who have the same disease (Hashimotos), seem to have different foods that help them feel their best and overcome the symptoms. In her situation, even when she eats "everything right" according to several different sources, she still can't lose weight (though that is not the main reason she eats healthy food). Her body's hormones refuse to let go of fat cells for whatever reason. She does what other people do to lose weight, yet for her it remains. She is in the process of figuring out how she is "like no others" and what will help her unique system to lose the extra weight, but if she tries to base her ideal diet on someone else's just because it helped them lose weight, she becomes frustrated.

---

[106] Experience used with permission, wishes to remain anonymous
[107] The resulting inflammation from *Hashimoto's* disease, also known as *chronic* lymphocytic *thyroiditis*, often leads to an underactive *thyroid* gland according to the Mayo Clinic.

No matter how wonderful your diet is for you, it may not be the best for someone else. No matter how wonderful your neighbor looks and feels, his diet may wreak havoc on your body. That is why we draw on the wisdom of multiple sources for help and glean the truth from whatever we learn. "Ultimately, the most reasonable view is this: Diet will vary from person to person, from one week to the next, and no matter what happens, nothing will stay the same for long."[108]

Your food diary is a good place to start to help you discover what you need. There you have before you data that shows at least in part what food makes you feel tired, sick, irritated, how long you go before you start to feel low-blood sugar symptoms, what foods were hard or easy to digest. Look to your food diary for ways you are like no others.

Metabolic Needs

In addition to a food diary, you could write down what your metabolic needs are. The unique and complex workings of one person will require a bit of trial and error to get right. I have heard that probiotics are helpful for people (like all others) because we all need healthy strains of bacteria in our systems. The gastroenterologist advised me to take probiotics because they are particularly helpful for people with IBS (like some others). I took one type from the drug store that caused me to break out in hives, one type from an natural oils company that seemed to do nothing at all, and fermented foods came with drawbacks, i.e. eating yogurt was just too high in lactose (even plain) or added sugars (like no others).

The probiotic that noticeably had a positive effect on my system, decreasing bloating and enhancing regularity in bowel movement, was kefir. Kefir has been a blessing for my health, and I've been tempted to tell everyone I meet with any sort of problem to eat kefir, but I remind myself that advice just doesn't work that way. My miracle probiotic may not work the same for you; it is your body, you must make your own observations.

---

[108] Marc David *Nourishing Wisdom*

Balance

Be sure to address every potential health issue, although you may not know you have more than one. When I tried to address just one problem, the blood sugar dysregulation, using all kinds of well meaning advice from people with the same problem, I still had many negative health problems. I wasn't addressing the unique combination of having IBS and low stomach acid in addition to problems regulating my blood sugar. I have to eat foods with complex molecules, proteins, and fiber, so as to not spike my blood sugar and insulin, yet my bowels have difficulty digesting foods with large complex molecules, particularly fat, and too much fiber. I've had to create a whole world of "balanced diet" that works for me, and even then that changes with the seasons and needs of my changing body.

Find the balance that works for you as far as food corruptions go. You can't fight them all, but at least you know they are not what your body needs. Set your boundaries, eliminate what you can, and notice when your body is signaling it needs an adjustment (i.e. depending on where your body is you may need more or less protein, vegetables or simple carbohydrates).

Love Your Food

While creating your ideal diet lifestyle, consider that it is not just *what* you eat but *how* you eat that is important. Stress, judgment, and fear will try to creep into your eating lifestyle. That only causes more problems, maybe as many problems as overeating sugar! Do not eat with fear; eat with love!

Somehow we must take responsibility for what we eat, and at the same time love ourselves, our food, and those around us. "We don't just hunger for food alone. We hunger for the experience of it— the tasting, the chewing, the sensuousness, the enjoyment, the textures, the sounds, and the satisfaction. If we continually miss these experiences, we will naturally want to eat again and again, but will remain unfulfilled."[109] Give your body what it needs by mindfully loving your life (taking responsibility) and your food (enjoy what you choose to eat).

I'm giving you permission to let it go! Listen to your body, ask your body if you need or even want to eat that particular food, savor what you do choose to eat, and learn from what response it gives you after you're finished.

Incorporate Pleasure into Your Ideal Diet

When we are doing our whole food challenges there is a measure of eliminating pleasure from eating, so we can get our systems to a place where we can find pleasure in eating healthful food. However, now I'm suggesting that you do not eliminate all pleasure from eating. As you make your optimal diet lifestyle, it's important to make sure you are putting in foods you love. Be careful not to think, "I can *only* eat to live, and I can *never* live to eat." Emily Rosen from the Psychology of Eating Institute explains why.

Your relationship with food has to do with how you assimilate, digest, and absorb it. I was so neurotic about food that I used to think, "Anything that tastes good I have to cut it out of my life." I got to a point where I thought I had to eat to live instead of live to eat. There is some significance and validity to that. The downside is when you do that intense and severe restriction and don't enjoy anything you eat, inevitably you are going to binge. Pleasure is a metabolic enhancer, which means it catalyzes the relaxation response. A meal that is completely devoid of pleasure and fun is not sustainable and not life affirming. We crave it, we need it, and if we deny ourselves of it, the healthy habits will be driven by negative reasons and won't be effective long term.[110]

In my ideal diet, I make sure to prepare my healthy meals in ways I can enjoy them. I don't drink a lot of green smoothies, even

---

[109] Marc David *Nourishing Wisdom*
[110] Emily Rosen, at the "Future of Healing" conference, June 22, 2015.

though some people swear by them, because I don't enjoy them and it's miserable to choke them down. I eat a lot of salads instead because I enjoy salads. I don't eat brownies, but I often enjoy a good chocolate date pecan roll. Dates taste very sweet to me and are enjoyable. I still make my own organic popcorn with healthy oils to enjoy with my movies. I love a good homemade loaf of gluten free bread. I make peach French toast and blueberry waffles, and I enjoy them! I'm not deprived of pleasure, and you shouldn't be either. Balance that "natural man" desire to splurge and that disciplined, cautious desire to eat clean, so you aren't abusing the food, and the food is giving back some joy.

Relationship with Food

Someone once asked me *in an ideal world, what would your relationship with food look like?* My answer was, in an ideal world, there wouldn't be food corruptions. People would grow food themselves and eat food the way God intended it to be eaten—whole and not refined—and people would not add things to it that kill organisms. We need the insects, the birds, the dirt, and the work it takes to eat, but in today's world the "Earth's Garden" has become corrupt. But since this is the time I live in, I will have a lifelong relationship with food and its corruptions. My relationship with food looks like a relationship with an imperfect person whom I love. If you substitute "be married" or "my spouse" into this paragraph wherever it says "to eat" or "food," you will see what I mean:

Blog post June 2015:

I love to eat, but sometimes I have negative feelings towards food. I enjoy making food, but it's the hardest work I do. I want to eat, but I look forward to the day where there aren't so many corruptions that make it so difficult. I'm doing my best to make sure it is helping and not hurting me by keeping healthy boundaries around what I eat. I'm trying to make sure I'm not eating to compensate for some other loss in my life. I'm trying to be careful how I treat food, and at the same time choosing food that gives back to me a healthful, pleasurable experience that will lift me up instead of drag me down. I try to remember that even though it's not always easy making food, it will bring me the most joy in the long term when I do it right.

That is an ideal relationship with food.

Spiritual Principle 6: Repentance

I hesitated to use the word *repent* in my book as it can make people feel judged or guilty of some terrible sin, and my book addresses weaknesses and misperceptions rather than deliberate sins. However, after one lesson I had the privilege to attend during Sunday School—which was about repentance—I felt I should use this specific principle. The instructor said one thing that bothered him most about being bishop was that people did not really understand repentance, viewing it as "time in jail," which a serious study of doctrine proves is not so.[111] Rather, repentance is a gift—the privilege of reconciling with our perfect and divine Father in Heaven—given to us through the enabling atonement of Christ. Repentance turns us toward the Father.

The word *repentance* according to the Bible Dictionary is defined as, "The Greek word of which this is a translation denotes a change of mind, i.e., a fresh view about God, about oneself, and about the world." I was surprised when I started this journey that I felt God saying to me, "Your sins are forgiven." Not that I believe eating unhealthy is necessarily a sin, rather, I felt God was communicating to me that by being disciplined and learning how to better take care of my physical temple, I was being refined and purified in ways I didn't understand and realize. When I thought about how changing my relationship with food turned me toward God and cleansed my body, that I was choosing to have "eyes that see and ears that hear" it made sense that I was, in a way, repenting.

---

[111] Lesson given by Randy Rogers

Our bodies are sacred temples, and God provides us food that is custom designed for our bodies to ingest. There is spiritual meaning to eating when you understand this. Eating wisely can be a way of choosing liberty and eternal life, and eating unhealthy foods can be viewed as captivity.[112] Trying to attain the "perfect" diet is not possible, just as being a perfect person is not possible, yet some measure of choice and accountability on our part is required for our body's health. As my instructor quoted: "Perfection is the goal, but direction is the test."[113]

Mosiah 3:19 reads: "For the natural man is an enemy to God, and has been since the fall of Adam, and will be forever and ever unless he yields to the enticings of the holy spirit, and putteth off the natural man and becometh a saint through the Atonement of Christ the Lord..."[114] I believe when you do something difficult to refine your body and spirit, thus bridling your passions, the Lord notices. He notices that you have a fresh view about God, about yourself, and about the world, and he forgives any past misperception or weakness you may have had.

> What fruit had ye then in those things whereof ye are now ashamed? for the end of those things is death.
> But now being made free from sin, and become servants to God, ye have your fruit unto holiness, and the end everlasting life.
> For the wages of sin is death; but the gift of God is eternal life through Jesus Christ our Lord.
> Romans 6:21-23

Challenge 6: Your Ideal Diet

With the seven-day and ten-day food challenges of chapters four and five in your mind, answer these questions in your journal:

---

[112] The Book of Mormon, 2nd Nephi 2:26
[113] Quote is from Robert Millet, professor emeritus BYU religion department
[114] The Book Of Mormon, Mosiah 3:19

- What food habits made you feel the best?
- What food habits made you feel the worst?
- What triggers/cravings/mind chatter did you discover?
- What opposition did you face?
- In what ways are you like all others, like some others, like no others?
- What are your unique health challenges and metabolic needs?
- What do you feel the Spirit is asking you to do?

Now, using the template below, write what an ideal diet would look like for you. Adjust it according to your needs and schedule. Make it something you would want to follow for life, allowing for some flexibility as you continue to experiment, refine, and improve your eating lifestyle.

My Optimal Diet Lifestyle Template

- In general, incorporate:
- Foods to avoid:
- How to eat:
- What times to eat what:
- Splurging is:

My Optimal Diet Lifestyle Template

In General: Incorporate balance of organic, whole, vegetables, fruits, and grains, grass fed non chemically treated beef, free range chickens, seafood, fermented foods, and supplements I feel my body may be in need of in the season my body calls for them.

Foods to Avoid: All forms of beet and cane sugar, corn syrup, wheat based flour, or other covert sugars, heavy fats and fatty proteins (i.e. bacon), unhealthy oils, and foods laden with antibiotic/preservatives.

How to eat: Mindfully, sitting up straight, chewing carefully, aware of my food and how it tastes, aware of how full I am, listening to my body, grateful for the life the food is giving me.

What times to eat what: Upon arising something that does not metabolize quickly or create an insulin response, like almonds or vegetables. Within two hours of arising a high protein breakfast and avoid grains in general in the morning. Four hours after breakfast combination of heavy molecules and whole simple carbs like potatoes, corn, oats. Four hours later snack or dinner, including fermented food. Before bed light whole food carb.

Splurging is: eating potato or corn chips, dried fruit, processed meats (i.e. hotdogs) or occasional sauce in a food that is served to me (i.e. mayonnaise in a chicken salad), or eating foods during other times than optimal due to circumstances.

Chapter 7: Vitality, a Choice

"A firm, unchangeable course of righteousness through life is what secures to a person true intelligence."

Brigham Young

Making a Case for Going Healthy for Good

When I was probably four or five years old, I have a memory of going to my paternal grandparents' home to visit with my great-grandparents who were there. My great-grandfather, who was blind and had his legs amputated below the knee, sat in his wheel chair with a blanket over his lap. I remember feeling badly for him, and I stood next to him for a long time staring at his unseeing eyes. I must have been very quiet for he didn't know I was there until someone said, "Grandpa, there's a child next to you!" He startled and felt around for me, but I had shyly leapt back to my mom's side by then. I remember wishing I had stayed there so he could touch me. I don't know if I ever did touch him. He died not long after that.

My great-grandfather suffered from diabetes. High blood sugar took his vision, took his legs, and eventually took his life. He lived a relatively long time despite it, and I believe this is because he was a hard working farmer who mostly ate what he harvested. His granddaughter, my aunt Kris, was not so lucky.

My father's sister Kris contracted diabetes when she was sixteen years old. She had a sweet tooth, so they tell me. But I know others who have eaten sugary sweets without restraint that did not contract diabetes at so young an age, so it may be more to do with her genetic vulnerabilities than eating habits. I'd like to believe that if large amounts of sugar weren't so available to her she may have lived longer, but that is conjecture. What I do know is that diabetes ravaged her body, and despite taking insulin faithfully all her life, she slowly lost function of her organs due to irregularities in blood sugar. Her eyesight, her kidneys, her feet; she suffered greatly because of the disease. At age forty-three she passed away.

Kris' father, my grandfather, contracted type two diabetes in his mid-late years. He died at about age seventy-two from complications to diabetes and cancer.

My uncle Ron, Kris' brother, contracted diabetes as a young man and died of a heart attack, most likely caused by complications to diabetes. My family members showed great patience in their afflictions. I loved them, and I have often wondered if it weren't for so many food corruptions increasing with the generations, if my aunt and uncle would have suffered less or may still be alive.

- **Prevalence**: In 2012, 29.1 million US citizens, or 9.3% of the population, had diabetes.
- Approximately 1.25 million US children and adults have type 1 diabetes.
- **Undiagnosed**: Of the 29.1 million, 21.0 million were diagnosed, and 8.1 million were undiagnosed.
- **Prevalence in Seniors**: The percentage of US citizens age 65 and older remains high, at 25.9%, or 11.8 million seniors (diagnosed and undiagnosed).
- **New Cases**: The incidence of diabetes in 2012 was 1.7 million new diagnoses/year; in 2010 it was 1.9 million.
- **Prediabetes**: In 2012, 86 million US citizens age 20 and older had prediabetes; this is up from 79 million in 2010.
- **Deaths**: Diabetes remains the 7th leading cause of death in the United States in 2010, with 69,071 death certificates listing it as the underlying cause of death, and a total of 234,051 death certificates listing diabetes as an underlying or contributing cause of death.

Generations Affected

According to data from the National Diabetes Statistics Report, 2014, diabetes is a huge problem in our country (see call out box on the previous page).[115] Had I not read the warning signs my body was giving me and intervened in my diet, would I be among the numbers in these statistics? Based on my family history, it is very likely. I don't want to give up fighting for a cause that could reverse the trend of increasing numbers afflicted by it. Especially since my family members died because of it, and my children could be victims of it.

The concept of biogenealogy suggests we pass not only our genes, but also our emotions, our addictions, our vulnerabilities, and our strengths on to the next generation.[116] When you choose to take a stand and live clean and healthy lives, you are not only sparing yourself needless pain, you are safeguarding generations to come. When you give in to bodily appetites and passions, you are inadvertently putting your children at a disadvantage at an emotional and cellular level. Every time I see people weakening their bodies with unhealthy eating habits, especially the overconsumption of sugar, I wish to share this information with the world!

Why Fight This?

Many experts[117] are saying that Type II Diabetes is not a diagnosis you have to live with. It's preventable and reversible if you make lifestyle changes. The paradigm of healing is changing! Now

---

[115] Data from the National Diabetes Statistics Report, 2014 (released June 10, 2014) - See more at: http://www.diabetes.org/diabetes-basics/statistics/

[116] Biogenealogy explained by Marc David in lecture with Sean Croxton June 2015.

[117] Brian Mowll, MD. Host of Diabetes Summit, drmowll.com, in conversation with Marc David in "Future of Healing" conference 2015. This assertion also made by Dr. David Perlmutter and Dr. Robert Lustig.

the frontier of healing is to understand gut micro biome.[118] Because the cornerstone of degenerative diseases such as heart disease, diabetes, and dementia is inflammation, and the bacteria contained in the gut play a pivotal role as to how much inflammation is in your body, we can reverse or prevent the damage by understanding and balancing gut bacteria. There are powerful approaches we can take now. It has been discovered that the balance of gut bacteria also has a role to play in depression, which influences our risk for any number of neurodegenerative diseases. Healthful eating is a leverage point that opens up the door to treatment possibilities.[119]

This is a revolutionary time for understanding human illness. I have a passion to help others heal their minds and bodies through eating healthful foods because it will make us stronger. I may not be able to prevent a car accident, but I can prevent and even reverse the premature weakening of my body!

Created to Have Joy

I once had a client who commented that, "the thing about life is no one comes out of it alive." His point was that we are going to die one way or the other. Why worry about it so much? He was also severely depressed and hopeless. I was not able to help that particular client, and I've always felt badly about that. I've often pondered his discouraging words. We are going to suffer; we are going to die. Both occur whether we work to eat or whether we cut corners and get sick. Does which suffering road we take really matter?

I wouldn't be writing this book if I didn't believe it matters very much. God didn't put us on this Earth to just roll over and die when

---

[118] Dr. Marc David, Dr. David Perlmutter, Dr. Tom O'Bryan, Dr. Srini Pallay and others have spoken to this point.
[119] Dr. David Perlmutter in lecture series "The Future of Healing" June 2015, for more information see his book *Brain Maker*

things got tough. We are meant to have joy.[120] He wants to see what we are made of! I prayed that my client eventually got the help he needed to pull out of his dark depression and become the mighty oak he has the potential to become. Every generation gets stronger when we fight for our lives and what is right.

I'd like to illustrate this point by sharing a dream I once had of opening a door, seeing layers of fabric, and knowing that each layer represented a quality of life that I had inherited from past generations. I started out with basic survival instincts, and in every generation a new level of strength and understanding was added to my collective self. Every time I would pull back a layer of fabric I would be told what it represented: one was kindness, one was perseverance, love for children, greater empathy, gratitude for life, integrity, virtue, courage, etc. They went on and on until I felt someone say, "You are an evolutionary marvel."

The righteous works of our ancestors were "stepping stones for generations."[121] The Saints of the last days are the collective strength of our progenitors—strong and faithful people who have come before us. We work to develop qualities through discipline and sacrifice so we can pass that on for generations. This creates a fullness of joy.

Why It's Worth the Fight

An example of facing pain for the benefit of future generations is illustrated in *The Book of Mormon*. In 1st Nephi, we read of the Lord commanding Lehi to take his family into the wilderness rather than stay in Jerusalem and be destroyed. If you think about it, why would the Lord ask him to do that? In the words of my client, we are all going to "perish" eventually. Why not stay in your home, with your nice conveniences and riches, and enjoy whatever time you have left? Instead, they spent eight years in the wilderness suffering

---

[120] Book of Mormon, 2 Nephi 2:25
[121] Quote taken from LDS Hymn "They the Builders of the Nations"

so many afflictions they couldn't number them. In fact, one of them did die on the way, and Lehi died not long after their arrival in the Promised Land.

Laman and Lemuel constantly complained about it, saying in essence that it would have been better that they had stayed in Jerusalem rather than suffer. Laman even says, "It were better that [we] had died before coming out of Jerusalem rather than suffer these afflictions."[122] Is it better? Nephi constantly tried to persuade them to be wiser. "How is it that ye do not keep the commandments of the Lord? How is it that ye will perish, because of the hardness of your hearts?" he asks them. Nephi and his family members suffered just as much if not more than Laman, yet he believes God is delivering them from affliction instead. Why does Nephi see the pain and afflictions so differently from his brothers?

Pain Inevitable in a Hostile World

The difference is that Laman somehow thought he could escape pain. He saw afflictions as something that he shouldn't have to tolerate and his pain to be caused by everyone around him. In reality he was causing his own pain. His sense of entitlement, feeling he deserved better, inability to be led by others, lack of eternal perspective, lack of humility to submit to God's will, interest in pleasure over reverence, and anger when chastised all caused him to feel more afflicted than he actually was. His determination to hate instead of love ended up affecting generations of his descendants (Lamanites), until a few brave missionaries decided they would "face pain and affliction" in order to bring the truth back to them.

It is not necessarily always easy to eat food that is healthy for you. In fact, it can sometimes feel like you are being punished for trying to do the right thing. This Earth life is not meant to be easy. No one is going to roll out the red carpet for you; life is messy, life is difficult, and life is painful no matter how good you are, brave you

---

[122] The Book of Mormon, 1st Nephi 17:20

are, and faithful you are. God has designed it this way for a reason that I cannot attempt to decipher. However, I do know this: when you face your pain and move toward your righteous objectives nonetheless, without causing your own pain of resentment that you must do so, you are passing whatever test this Earth life was designed to give us.

Facing Pain Decreases Future Pain

Lehi's family's obedience to the commandment to flee Jerusalem gave generations of people the opportunity to live in a beautiful land. Their faith, strength, obedience, courage, and submission to afflictions ultimately resulted in *The Book of Mormon,* the keystone of The Church of Jesus Christ restored in the Latter days. Doing something difficult can result in unimaginable blessings.

I'm asking you to face some pain in order to relieve worse pain! Isn't that really what the Lord was asking Lehi? "Trust me, leave your riches, your comfort zone and wade through afflictions. If you go, you will eternally have more joy in seeing generations of your seed inherit the earth. If you stay, you would eternally have more pain in seeing your family cut off and destroyed completely." God blessed Lehi for his faith and trust.

The whole idea of *Wise Food Mind* is that if you can change your mind-set about food, and trust that change can and needs to happen, you will be blessed. Your eating habits for life will improve, your health will thrive, your ability to feel the spirit and progress spiritually will improve, and ultimately and eternally you will have less pain than before! That is why I am passionate about this cause.

Warning: Many will Defend Old Ways

Be prepared to face another pain: those who question your resolve. "At every crossway on the road that leads to the future, each progressive spirit is opposed by a thousand men appointed to defend the past."[123] Anyone who has been healed by changing food habits knows it's real, but there will be many who insist that diet has little to do with health, or scoff at the idea that you can listen to your body for the answers instead of going to the doctor. Some may even be offended at the suggestion that their cake and ice cream had anything to do with their heart problems, headaches, joint pain, mood dysregulation, etc. I've had to bite my tongue at times as I've interacted with those who are not ready to hear the truth and who make comments about why I should relax and enjoy food. But don't let that stop *you*! You have the solution. Your gut can be healed. No matter what it takes, never give up!

Some may also raise the valid point that the human body is hard wired to avoid pain and seek pleasure, and to relieve suffering is to eliminate or avoid pain. I don't believe we need to actively seek out painful, difficult experiences because its "good for the soul." I do believe that trying to avoid or ignore problems will only make worse problems. It is better to face pain in the short run to avoid more pain in the long run. Remember the Lord's counsel that "the natural man is an enemy to God," and doing something right, even if your nature was not programmed to do it, can actually be "putting off the natural man and becoming a Saint through the Atonement of Christ."[124]

Long Term Benefits of Nutrition

According to the nutritionists and experts, in improving my diet I'm gaining long-term health benefits such as reduced risk for heart disease, Alzheimer's, diabetes, cancer, and more.[125] I am changing my gene expression and becoming stronger. I am saving my children from a compromised micro biome and preventing future disease for

---

[123] Maurice Maeterlinck, 1900's Nobel Laureate, quoted by David Perlmutter

[124] The Book of Mormon, Mosiah 3:19

[125] David Perlmutter, Robert Lustig, Mark Hyman, Marc David, Diane Sanfilippo, Tom O'Bryan, and more.

them as well. I may never know how many long-term benefits I am gaining by limiting my intake of food toxins, but I know there are some other interesting benefits I've noticed right now!

I never had hard or defined muscles until I cleaned up my diet. That may sound like a strange long-term benefit to ring up, but it was fascinating to me to have muscle definition. At age thirty-seven I had strength in my calves, thighs, and arms I'd never had before. I'd lived my whole life without that and never knew it could be different.

I can exercise and enjoy it. I hiked up to the G on the mountainside behind our home one morning, and thought about how hard it was for me to hike the mountain behind our house the last summer when I was still healing from years of sugar abuse. This hike was glorious and delightful, despite it being completely straight up for 85% of the hike!

I don't get sick on a regular basis anymore. I used to get migraines once a month at least, sometimes more. In fact, head pain isn't really a problem now. I haven't taken a pain killer for head pain for over a year. I rarely get head colds. My nose used to be a faucet that gave me only brief reprieves in between whatever new bug I'd caught. Now I'm rarely afflicted by colds.

I don't worry about having depression anymore. If I'm exhausted, cry about things, and even behave irrationally and moody, the next morning I'm fine. There aren't residual negative feeling that follow me or a heavy feeling of despair in the morning. I still get sad and discouraged sometimes, or angry and frustrated, but my ability to process emotions and let them go is exponentially improved. Subsequently, my ability to help others process their emotions has also improved.

The best long term benefit I feel I have gained is a clear mind. This way I can be the recipient of truth and can better ward off the negative influence of the adversary. We can sometimes be in quite a conundrum down here. For example, when we do what is right Satan makes us feel terrible about it or has us questioning our worth and intentions, masking the love and pleasure God is trying to communicate to us. If we do what is wrong, Satan makes us feel terrible about it and guilt can cause us quite a bit of emotional pain, overriding the appropriate feelings of remorse from our conscience that can lead to repentance and change. With a clear intellect, you can discern between the Spirit and the adversary and lessen the possibility of creating your own pain.

Having a clear intellect helps me accept God's will and be not troubled. It helps me recognize His hand in directing my life, and it helps me have strength and courage to carry on, all the while enhancing a love for others and warding off selfish desires and actions. Before I was healed, it was difficult to go on another day let alone have these righteous desires and motives! You too will be in a position to model righteous behavior, serve others, teach others the truth, and know the purposes God intends for you. Nourishing your body nourishes your spirit.

Long Term Benefits take a Long Time

At the risk of being redundant, I will say again change takes time. I want you to go healthy for good to give your body the time it needs to really heal, but that poses another obstacle in the process because many of us are used to getting things done quickly. Author Bradley Nelson said:

> The body sometimes needs help to restore itself to a state of balance. This help may consist of removing trapped emotions, detoxification, receiving chiropractic adjustments, proper nutrition, and more. Healing is a process, and it takes time. But waiting for the body to heal itself naturally can try our patience. We usually want a quick fix. We don't want to wait; we want it now.[126]

---

[126] Dr. Bradley Nelson. The Emotion code: How to Release Your Trapped Emotions for Abundant Health, Love and Happiness, Wellness Unmasked Publishing, 2007

Don't get caught up in the mindset that because things aren't all better after a week whatever you tried didn't work. Real healing just takes longer. Marc David is a doctor and psychologist who spent his life trying to learn how to heal people with nutrition. He told people what to eat, but people couldn't do it. People would tell him, "You told me I should eat this way and I tried it but nothing changed!" His response was, "You dabbled. If you want to learn anything, you train."

Real change requires frequency and intensity. So he developed an eating psychology program where people can change their relationship with food and practice what it takes to change. People want a quick fix, so a lot of people want to give up. If you can develop a mind shift from "I tried and failed" to "I failed the first week, but that's great because I tried!" your body can learn what it needs to really change. People give up too early. Keep failing and trying until you have a breakthrough.[127]

Splurging

Of course there will be times when you don't have as much control over what you eat. Even if you have control, getting to that place where you are eating pleasurable foods but not abusing food is tricky. That is why creating an ideal (albeit not perfect) diet is important. How do you know if you are splurging unless you have a solid and clear boundary about what ideal is in the first place? You don't!

If a person's ideal diet includes never eating food cooked in a microwave, a splurge would be going to grandma's and eating the soup she reheated. Heating your own soup in the microwave would not be a splurge. That would just be cheating or not sticking to your ideal diet, but your brain can't keep track of that unless you know what the boundaries are. I had one person tell me, "After reading

---

[127] Taken from lecture with Sean Croxton and Marc David in "Depression Sessions" June 2015. For more information, visit psychologyofeating.com

chapter six I realized my 'once in a while' splurges were out of control. I was doing it all the time because I didn't have a clear definition of what 'once in a while' even meant." Exactly!

Only you can define what ideal looks like. As stated in chapter six, it is OK to eat for pleasure, but we want healthful food to be the pleasurable food we desire. When you enjoy celery with almond butter or cinnamon on top of whole apples, you don't need to splurge on cakes, soda, and candy. When I have a weak moment and need comfort food, a whole date or banana oatmeal will do the trick. You need to clearly state what goes and what stays, what you can "splurge" on and what a splurge means for you.

Splurging is when you still stick hard to your "no list" but give in to your "on certain occasions" list. For example, I never eat desserts at restaurants or others' homes because I have to know exactly what kind of sweetener is used and how much of it is in each serving size, and the only way to do that is to make it myself. At home I make myself "treats" at times, but out and about it's a strict NO. At home, I try to be diligent about not ingesting unhealthy oils. (Soybean oil and vegetable oil are on my "only on certain occasions" list, I know they aren't good for me but they don't cause blood sugar dysregulation.) I avoid eating them at home in my controlled environment so that I can eat these oils when I go out to eat, because most restaurants cook their chips, tortillas, potatoes, vegetables, etc in vegetable/soybean oil. That helps me regulate it as an "only on certain occasions."

Cooking for Good

As you consider picking your day to go healthy for good, keep in mind that from that time forth you may well be cooking your own meals the majority of the time. Unless you hire a cook! There are a lot of benefits to cooking so keep an open mind as you learn the trade. If you need to extend the behavioral contract to thirty days, then three months, then one year before you go healthy for good, that is perfectly fine. It might help you to train your mind and body to prepare your own food.

Recipe Modifications

One of the secret keys of joyful cooking in my life has been the idea of recipe modification. You can make recipes you used to make if you modify it with healthful foods. For example, let's say you used to love Hawaiian haystacks, but because of the cream of chicken soup, gluten, and refined grains it's on your "no list." No problem! You can cook brown or wild rice (whole grains), and make your own chicken broth and gravy with corn flour (gluten free), and use nuts and seeds instead of oriental noodles for the crunchy topping (reducing simple carbs)! And enjoy all the whole food vegetable toppings you'd like. Yes, it takes longer, but you don't have to go without for the rest of your life. Check out this example:

Traditional Recipe for Peanut Butter Cookies

1 cup unsalted butter
1 cup crunchy peanut butter
1 cup white sugar
1 cup packed brown sugar
2 eggs
2 1/2 cups all-purpose flour
1 teaspoon baking powder
1/2 teaspoon salt
1 1/2 teaspoons baking soda

Cream butter, peanut butter, and sugars together in a bowl; beat in eggs. In a separate bowl, sift flour, baking powder, baking soda, and salt; stir into butter mixture. Put dough in refrigerator for 1 hour. Roll dough into 1 inch balls and put on baking sheets. Flatten each ball with a fork, making a crisscross pattern. Bake in a preheated 375 degrees F oven for about 10 minutes or until cookies begin to brown.

Modified Recipe for Peanut Butter Cookies

2 cups organic fresh ground peanut or almond butter
1/4-1/2 cup organic grade B maple syrup or organic honey, or no
sweetener for pure sugar free option
1/2 cup oats
2 tsp baking powder
3 eggs
1/2 tsp salt
1 tsp vanilla powder

Mix together peanut butter, syrup, oats, eggs, baking powder and salt
with electric mixer. Spoon tablespoon size dollops onto baking sheet
covered with wax paper. Press down with greased spatula to flatten.
Bake at 375 degrees for 8-10 minutes.

    *   *   *   *   *   *

About now you may be saying, "That is so much harder than
you make it sound." But remember we gave up convenience. Those
days are behind us now! We are ready to get our hands in the fridge
and do what it takes to eat nourishing and beneficial food for life. It
is "food love" on a whole new level. Love is a choice, an action, and
shows respect. You love food and you love life! Let's respect both
and choose to act wisely about eating.

How to Simplify

Just living in the United States means many things are already
simplified. My father worked with a woman from Russia, who came
to the United States for a better life. She told my father that she loved
America because there were so many conveniences! In Russia, after
they worked all day, they came home and had to slaughter, clean,
pluck, season, and cook their chicken, and after about three hours of
preparation you had a meal. She stated that she was amazed that you
could go to the store and buy a chicken ready to eat. There is some
merit to that. In many ways we have it easy here, and we already
take advantage of many ways to simplify.

Many farmers markets and natural food stores have organic food ready for you to consume. We don't have to harvest all our food. It is wonderful if you can have a garden, chickens, and fresh eggs, but if you do not, there are many others that do and we can support them. Being a wise consumer means you choose the foods that are made from wise producers, who do not add harmful things to their produce or animal feed. If we all start buying wisely, more demand will cause more people to produce, and it will become more abundant. Hopefully then the mass produced processed food will become less abundant.[128]

Pre-making food at the beginning of the week is a great way to simplify. Salads can be prepared, sealed, and kept crisp in the fridge for five days. When you prepare a chicken or turkey, you can put some meat away, or even use the bones to make broth for another meal. Cook double portions so you can have leftovers the next day. Some work is still involved, but after you get the theory behind simplifying, you can create your own symphonies of easy meals.

Budget Constraints

The unfortunate fact that fresh organic food is more expensive than corrupt mass produced food can be a hindrance to many people. Price matching and couponing will not get you very far with high quality, whole food. It is expensive to keep animals. You can buy a lot of organic eggs for the price of raising chickens. Just as we want good quality food more abundantly produced, we want it affordable as well! Again, if wise consumers will stop buying the cheap stuff so that more support will be given to sell more high quality food, thereby increasing the supply for the demand, this could lower costs.

However, if you have tight funds, you may have to choose your battles. Maybe you won't be able to buy organic eggs, but you can buy brown or wild rice and grind your own rice flour. It is an

---

[128] Youtube "Sugar is Killing Us" campaign video, https://www.youtube.com/watch?v=Yda8RtOcVFU

investment to buy kitchen aides and higher quality food, but a wise one. Even if you can't afford it now, you can set some money aside to use when you can.

It is important to keep in mind that if you eat cheap now, you may be paying later in the form of medical bills or being sick and staying home from work. Paying a little more to buy food that is truly nourishing is another way to "eat thy bread by the sweat of thy brow." If you can't garden yourself, use the money you worked for to support those who produce organically and locally.

Picky Eaters

If a child is refusing to eat anything but refined or sugary food, it is an indication that their micro biome has no or limited bacterial strains that craves or are accustomed to other types of food. It is a battle of patience. Introducing foods that help them and limiting foods that hurt them will be more difficult, and you may feel like a sculptor chipping away at a mountain trying to create a sculpture. Keep chipping away. There is so much evidence today that improving diet improves child health and brain function, it is worth the effort. A little pain now saves us a lot of pain later.

Other Conundrums

The school lunch system has not yet found a way to serve masses of children anything other than frozen, canned, shelved, and otherwise processed foods. You will need to make your kids' lunches if you want to

School Lunch Ideas
Monday: chicken salad with homemade dressing and homemade granola bars
Tuesday: tuna and pickles , homemade potato chips, and cinnamon almond butter with apples
Wednesday: potato cubes and chicken sausage, celery with almond butter
Thursday: gluten free bread turkey/chicken sandwiches and snap peas
Friday: cheese squares, cut beef franks, and grapes

steer clear of gluten, sugar, chemicals, and additives. A lunch bag with an ice pack option is a good idea to keep lunches that are homemade cool. Ideas for lunches are listed in the call out box.

Allow your children to have a say in what you put in their lunch. When children feel different, (i.e. others saying, "Gross, what is that in your lunch!") or weird they will not care how harmful school lunch is or healthy their lunch is. Children will beg you to put in a marshmallow peanut-butter white bread sandwich in their lunch so they can be like everyone else. Inquire, empathize, and collaborate on what to make for lunches.

Other challenges you may face are campouts, eating at grandma's, vacations, and holidays. My Thanksgiving of 2014 was a salad that I brought and some turkey. Everything else was made with something I was trying to avoid for my health. You may have to bring something you can eat when you visit people or attend family dinners.

You will definitely want to pack your own camping cooler. I collaborated with a neighbor to make a week long menu of gluten-free, sugar-free meals for both our daughters at girls' camp. It was extra work, but my daughter felt great the whole week, which was well worth my effort. And it showed to her that I am serious about protecting her gut and brain.

Going Out to Eat

Eating out is a great break from cooking your own food all day. There are many places that do not have health conscious food options on their menu. I would just avoid those places as you avoid other food corruptions. But there are many places that have healthful alternatives and are happy to accommodate people with special diets. Restaurants with salad bars are nice because you have lots of options for whole foods. Research or experiment to find places that you feel good about.

Going out may be when you splurge, which is fine as long as you have a boundary with it. I have a solid boundary that I do not buy desserts or drinks when I go out, but I do splurge on trans fat items like chips and fries. Making sure that I don't over-eat when going out helps me digestively. There is always the "doggie bag" you can take extra food home in.

Mindful Eating

I'd like to re-emphasize the importance of not only guarding what you eat, but how you eat. Slow down when you eat. Mindful eating is to sit down, sit up straight, chew your food, think about how it tastes, and savor the experience of eating.[129] This will help you stay in "rest and digest" mode, and will help your body feel full, preventing any tendency to over-eat. Allow your body the satisfaction and joy of eating mindfully.

Spiritual Principle 7: Patience

It takes as long as it takes. We have all heard the parable of the ten virgins and understand that being prepared for the second coming requires having our own individual spiritual fuel or "oil in our lamps." How do we keep our lamps full of oil? Obedience to commandments over a lifetime. That takes some patience! Spencer W. Kimball explains:

> In the parable, oil can be purchased at the market. In our lives the oil of preparedness is accumulated drop by drop in righteous living. Attendance at sacrament meeting adds oil to our lamps, drop by drop over the years. Fasting, family prayer, home teaching, *control of bodily appetites,* preaching the gospel, studying the scriptures—each act of dedication and obedience is a drop added to our store.[130]

---

[129] Pavel G. Somov, "360 degrees of mindful eating" seminar 2009.
[130] Spencer W. Kimball from *Faith Precedes the Miracle* [1972], 256, quoted in LDS New Testament Sunday School Manual

Control of bodily appetites is an important way to be prepared. Not just for thirty days, for as long as we are alive or until the second coming, we prepare and wait. We put forth effort to improve to qualify for blessing of Atonement and come forth in the morning of the first resurrection. No more sitting around letting life happen to you, tolerating whatever time is left before you perish. Your determination to do what is right will affect generations after you. It will not only add oil to your lamp, but fill oil barrels in the storage shed for generations of worthy people who will find easier access to filling their own lamps as they prepare for the future as well.

> Do ye suppose that God will look upon you as guiltless while ye sit still and behold these things? Behold I say unto you, Nay. Now I would that ye should remember that God has said that the inward vessel shall be cleansed first, and then shall the outer vessel be cleansed also.
>
> And now, except ye do repent of that which ye have done, and begin to be up and doing...
>
> I will leave the strength and the blessings of God upon [you], that none other power can operate against [you]—
>
> And this because of [your] exceeding faith, and [your] patience in tribulations.
>
> Alma 60:23-25

Patience: there will come a time you won't even miss those foods that have been a comfort to you for years. Obey what you know to be right. It is time to make the body an instrument rather than a master of the spirit.[131]

Challenge 7: Healthy for Good

You have your optimal diet lifestyle worked out. You have learned what it takes to make it happen and why make it happen. Now *choose* to have a Wise Food Mind. Pick a day when you will eat healthfully from that time forth. Remember your food diary, your

---

[131] Quoted by D. Todd Christofferson, April 2015 General Conference

thought records, and your gathered knowledge—you know what to abstain from and what to incorporate in order to start a new food way of life. Now drum up all your faith, patience, obedience, and gratitude, and no matter what forces oppose you, take a stand for your health and your life.

My Day of Deliverance:

Chapter 8: Educating Children

The biggest effort we could make to collectively heal our nation is having mothers teach children about love and good food. Giving kids Snickers is not love. Making something from fresh ingredients, that is love. The lesson has to be taught in the home.

Peter Osborne[132]

Raising a Clean Generation

Congratulations! You have begun training your brain and body to love food that nourishes you. The next step is to help your kids adjust as well. You may have already changed their diets along with yours (no parent likes to make two meals at meal time to appease the picky eaters), so some of this may already be happening. This is a new kind of hard on a number of levels.

I have three children. They each have unique experiences with setting healthy boundaries with food. They are not in any way deprived. We have been blessed financially to always have enough money for buying plenty of healthy, organic, whole produce, meat, grains, and many natural sweeteners and herbs. They have a mother who is willing to make food for them breakfast, lunch, and dinner and who teaches them how to make their own food as well. I teach them what I know and allow them to make their own choices about what to eat. However, each has their own difficulties with re-training their brain and gut to eat food that benefits instead of deprives them.

Different Metabolic Needs Even Within Families

My oldest and youngest have minimal immediate side effects from food corruptions. My oldest has mild weight gain issues and mood swings when she eats sugary refined foods, and my youngest

---

[132] Quote from lecture "Clinical Nutrition and Pastoral Health" June 2015. For more information go to drpeterosborne.com and myfunctionalmedicinedoctor.org

throws up when he eats too much soybean oil. So their personal resolve to eat healthfully is low, although sometimes they refrain to please me. I don't buy it and don't serve it, but sometimes they indulge in refined foods and sugar at church, school, and others' homes where it is abundant.

My oldest does not care for the taste of some vegetables and whole foods. She was trained from infancy to have processed and high sugar content foods, so she struggles to eat food just because it is good for you. She only feels satisfied when what she eats is enjoyable and plentiful. I don't want her to feel like she is living a life of deprivation, and I don't want her to feel compelled to sneak around! However, I also don't want her brain and gut trained to think that only food she craves and desires are what she needs to eat.

My youngest is very active and it seems he can eat nearly anything without any problems. However, his desire to please me and do the right thing motivates him to not complain at home, not sneak around, and show moderation when he does splurge. I've noticed when he has a chance to eat "bad food," he does so quickly and is careful to not let me see him. This makes me sad, because I don't want him to associate guilt with eating. If he is going to indulge I want him to enjoy it!

Both their difficulties in keeping healthy boundaries with food pricks my conscience—am I doing them harm instead of good? This is another level of difficult! I want to give up and just tell them to enjoy it and eat for pleasure. Yet I know that though the consequences are unapparent at this time, allowing, supporting, or encouraging them to eat whatever they want whenever they want can cause long-term problems. I set up some boundaries and restrictions so that when my children gain a personal resolve to have food boundaries, they will know what to do.

My middle child is a different story. She has IBS, blood sugar regulation issues, a sweet tooth (or sugar addiction), and feels sick when she has too much unhealthy oils, gluten, sugar, and milk. After

I cleaned up our diet, she noticed very quickly when she ate elsewhere what food corruptions make her feel sick. For example, when she went to Clear Creek Camp during the summer for five days, she suffered a major headache the entire time she was there and came home sick. Her metabolic type was obviously highly sensitive to the high amounts of refined carbs, sugar, toxic oils, and gluten they fed the kids while there for breakfast, lunch, and dinner. It took her a few times of giving in to her desire for sweets and bread and feeling sick before she decided she was going healthy for good.

Now that she is eating clean, I've noticed that *I* find it difficult in situations when my other two kids and my husband are eating without restraint, like at the breakfast buffet at our camp resort where they ate cinnamon rolls and waffles with strawberries and cream while she and I just ate our eggs and potatoes and sipped water. This is a whole new level of mind chatter screaming *It's not fair!* I want her to have cream and bread like everyone else. It was one thing for my body to be limited and need to be careful, now I have to watch my child endure it as well.

However, her body has indicated at a young age that she needs whole foods. I'm most concerned about how food corruptions will affect her because her addiction to sugar, IBS symptoms, and immediate negative health problems after eating certain foods are warning signs that something inside is suffering. According to her "food diary," she needs to be careful about what she takes in. I can't give up or let her give up because it hurts me to see her go without. I know it's not right. I applaud her efforts and success in loving her body enough to not harm it, and know my other two children are in their own ways making great efforts and will be successful as well.

Children Learn Eventually

If you don't give up there are some joyful rewards. My oldest has learned how to enjoy many healthful foods, my middle child has learned many gluten free recipe modifications, and my youngest has a greater appreciation when he does get sweets. They are all learning great life lessons like how to cook, to read labels, to stick to behavioral contracts. They have learned how to show gratitude instead of complain.

I let my girls fend for themselves one evening and they decided to cook dinner for the family. They grilled chicken sausage, fried green beans in avocado oil, and made mashed potatoes for us all. My husband and I were so grateful and impressed when we got home later that evening! How wonderful that they have developed the life skill to work to make themselves a whole food meal.

The DOs and DON'Ts

Whatever the case may be for your children, there are some Dos and Don'ts when it comes to getting your family on board with incorporating healthy food and eliminating food corruptions. What not to do:

1) If it is a food corruption, don't buy it and don't serve it!

2) Don't expect happy faces, thank yous, or support.

3) Don't give up even if at times you have to give in.

What to do:

1) Respect their agency; kids will need to have freedom to choose to effectively retrain their brains and guts.

2) Use effective parenting skills in implementation of new foods and educating children.

3) Love them no matter what.

Don't Buy It

I was surprised when I started eating whole foods just how many processed foods were in my home, mostly from my own decision to purchase them. When I started cooking only whole food meals, my husband and children turned to those sweet, processed, corrupt foods often and they didn't last long. Once they were gone, they were gone, and if you wanted to eat ketchup you had to make your own from scratch or have what Mom was cooking.

Children in general have a strong hunger instinct. There are very few children who will not eat something they don't like when hungry enough. I'm not suggesting you callously let them starve until they break down and eat what you serve. I am saying that it is OK to patiently let them refuse to eat sometimes when they are having a difficult time drumming up the courage to try something daunting. As long as you don't buy it and don't serve it, they won't be able to sneak after bed-time and eat corrupt food because they refused the good stuff. When their hunger instinct is strong enough, they will have more resolve to try something new.

They can try to find something else to eat, but if you haven't bought it, the food that hurts them won't be there. If they refuse to eat lunch and dinner, remember that a person can go twenty-four hours not eating without any danger to their body. In fact, some argue that fasting occasionally is quite healthy and necessary for good brain health.[133] The next morning when their strong hunger instinct kicks in, there is more momentum to try the eggs and grapefruit rather than cry because they can't have Eggo waffles anymore. And the retraining of a child's brain and gut begins.

Don't Expect Happy Faces

Remember those physical, emotional, and psychological withdrawals? The kids will have them too. But they won't be able to articulate or even recognize what is happening. All they know is that they feel angry and "life is not fair" because they can't have cereal or cake and ice cream on their birthday anymore. If we are going to expect anything, we should probably expect that your kids aren't going to be too happy for a three to eighteen months while their bodies adjust (recovered from sugar addiction and taste buds for certain foods develop and bacterial flora are created). Trust me, they won't starve.

---

[133] David Perlmutter *Grain Brain*

Children can be a powerful outside force to try and stop you from clearing up their food addictions. They may say mean and discouraging things, complain and cry often, or be made fun of by their peers. I know that I felt guilty and like I was causing everyone's misery. It takes some wise self-talk to stay committed.

Observe your mind chatter: What pain are you really interested in stopping, yours or theirs? Long term or short term? Are you wondering *am I depriving my kids?* Remember this is not about deprivation; it's about safety. You wouldn't give your kids poison/drugs/parasites (though large food corporations would). Our job as parents is to teach them consequences and model appropriate behavior. If you find it "too hard" to serve healthful food to your children and not give them treats, is it to appease your own pain or theirs?

Tell yourself that trying to keep food corruptions out of your children's diets is part of reversing the trend that the standard American diet started, not you, so there is no reason to feel guilt. Taking a stand and helping your child recover from food addictions is part of loving your kids by doing the right thing for them even if they don't like it. You wouldn't let them play in the busy street, play with fire, or swallow bathroom cleaner, would you? Even if they wanted to really badly? Of course not. You are doing the right thing, and I applaud your effort even if your children don't.

Don't Give Up

Since everyone is different, even your kids will have different dispositions and relationships with food. This can result in different struggles that will tempt you to give up because you had to give in. Try not to be too iron clad, rigid, or black and white about it. That may stir up negative emotions, interfere with attachment, undermine your efforts, or push them in the opposite direction. Sometimes giving in needs to happen so the child knows you love them, but you don't need to give up. Help them try again another time.

If the child chooses to give in that is one thing, but you do not need to give in. As time wears on, you will be tempted to let the kids splurge more often because it can be harder to watch your kids go without than it is to go without yourself. What parent (or what grandparent for that matter) doesn't love to give their child a treat to show their love? Now we know that is not love. That is reinforcing a negative eating habit. It may be painful to change this mindset.

Furthermore, children think in how-can-I-win terms, so don't get caught up in an argument defending your actions or demand gratitude for your efforts. Just empathize that it is hard and keep your expectations for support low until they are in a place where you can educate them on the importance of eating food that nourishes their bodies.

Do Respect Agency

My husband took our family camping recently at a cabin resort in the Sierra Nevada mountains. There was a horseback riding opportunity we took advantage of while we were there, and it was a highlight of the experience. The horses' owner asked which one of us was the most assertive, and I told them I probably was, so she put me on a special horse named Spot.

We all got saddled up and the owner gave us some riding instructions before we went on our excursion. She told us that the horses may try to eat some of the vegetation along the trail, but there are some poisonous plants that if eaten too much will kill the horses, so don't let them eat. If they try to eat, just pull up hard on the reins and kick their belly with your heals.

It didn't take me long to figure out why Spot needed an assertive rider. Not ten feet into the ride, Spot was eating the vegetation along the trail. I did what I was supposed to and pulled up on the reins, but Spot didn't care. After he got his bite he would walk along and a few steps later, he was eating again. My pulls started turning into yanks, but they didn't seem to have any effect on Spot. I started yanking and kicking as hard as I could but it was like he didn't even feel my kicks. It was only the willow switch from the guide behind us that would get him moving, even then only after he'd helped himself to the vegetation along the trail.

My slight and short body trying to get that big horse to do what he needed was quite comical I'm sure. I was really no match for him. I kept telling Spot, "You have to keep going, you can't eat those plants. They are poisonous! Besides you are going to get switched again! Don't you know what is good for you?" All I could do was try to communicate to him with the reins and my kicks that he was not to eat the plants, but nonetheless the horse had his agency. If he got sick from it, I had done all I could do.

Your children are also beings with agency, and we can't kick, yank, and switch them to get them to comply. Even if we teach, guide, direct, and correct the best possible way, they may still choose to "eat the poisonous grass," so to speak. Don't shame them, and don't take it personally. Their life experience is their own and one day when it becomes important enough to them, they will remember your direction.

Do Utilize Effective Parenting Skills

The five E's of Love and Logic are valuable in changing the diet and in teaching children about how to eat wisely.[134] These include empathy, example, experience, encouragement, and expectation. I'll discuss only three E's in detail here, but if you'd like more information the *Parenting with Love and Logic* books are well worth your time.

Example is simple, but crucial, and involves modeling the behavior you wish your children to engage in. You can't expect your children to do what you yourself are not doing. If you want your children to be honest, you need to model honesty. If you want them

---

[134] *Parenting with Love and Logic* by Jim Fay and Foster Cline

to be respectful to others, you must model respect for others yourself. A parent who throws swear words around at home should not be surprised when the teacher calls and says their son used the F word at them in class. Likewise, if you model inappropriate eating behaviors and habits, your children will likely follow those behaviors themselves.

Before you implement any diet lifestyle changes in your children's lives, make sure you are willing to follow the regime first. It would be extremely confusing to a child if you said you really shouldn't drink soda but on certain occasions you go ahead and drink soda. No matter how good the excuse or situation is, a child will simply internalize it as opportunity to justify their own actions on what they want to eat later.

Empathy is, in my opinion, the most important parenting skill one could have, and the most difficult to execute correctly. Empathy is to identify the underlying emotion of your child and validate it, even if you don't understand, agree, or like it. Instead of correcting or punishing the child for feeling a certain way, you try to take their perspective for a minute and communicate back to them that how they see things is true for them.

This can be extremely difficult to do genuinely. One look on your face that the child is being ridiculous can undermine efforts to be empathetic. Additionally, irrational, selfish, even cruel behavior of the child may make sorting out whatever underlying emotion exists and empathizing with it virtually impossible. It takes some practice, but is very valuable in connecting with your child and allowing them the opportunity to correct themselves, knowing you've "got their back."

For example, let's say you have just spent an hour making a whole food, nutrient dense, corruption-free meal for the family and your daughter comes up for breakfast. She sits at the table, where you have even plated her food for her, and instead of eating it she makes a sour face, takes a bite, then says she isn't hungry. You could:

A) Be exasperated and tell her you don't care that she doesn't like it. Lecture that food doesn't always have to taste amazing. It's good for her and if she doesn't eat that she doesn't eat at all.

B) Start to cry and tell her how ungrateful she is, and that you guess she doesn't want a personal cook after all and she can just cook her own food from now on.

C) Ignore her, put the food away, and buy her some fast food later.

D) Stay calm and take this opportunity to teach her about the dangers of the standard American diet.

E) Put your arm around her and recognize that she is feeling sad that she has to find the strength to eat something she doesn't really like or go hungry. Tell her "I know what that's like, and you're not alone."

To be honest, I've behaved in all these ways at one time or another with my children. As you can imagine, some do not have favorable results. What is the most empathetic response in this situation? Clearly, option E would be ideal. If she has someone to process the difficult emotion with and vent some negative mind chatter to, she may be able to drum up the strength to eat some of the food.

Encouragement is helpful in getting children moving in a certain direction. The Law of Behavioral Science asserts that all living creatures behave in the certain ways they do because that behavior is reinforced in some way. You can appreciate this because your old eating habits were reinforced by feeling good for a moment, filling a "fun void," and feeding a craving—all powerful reinforcements. You've spent a lot of time researching other reinforcements for helping you create new eating behaviors.

Encouragement is also a reinforcement. We all love to be noticed, recognized, or valued; we crave it as much as we crave sweet food. When you notice when a child does well at something, it gives them motivation to behave that way again to get further recognition.

Examples of encouragement include noticing when they make a wise choice, especially when they did it right on their own. You can say, "I notice that you chose to have a celery stick for a snack." You don't even have to say, "You are amazing" or "Good choice!" In fact, refraining from any judgment is sometimes the best call. You just have to notice it. Other encouraging things you can say are: "Thank you for tasting it." "I notice you didn't have a cookie at the party." "How did you get yourself to finish that?" Like empathy, encouragement fills a child's emotional love tank and gives their brain more motivation to make the effort to behave in those ways again in the future.

Do Love Your Children

I've heard it said that parenting can be boiled down into three key elements: 1) I love you, 2) If you have any questions, ask, and 3) Good luck in life.[135] This formula emphasizes the importance of love. If you don't love your kids, all the best parenting advice in the world isn't going to help you.

Love is a loaded word. The dictionary defines love as "a feeling of warm personal attachment or deep affection, as for a parent, child, or friend." I agree. When clients come to me with parent-child or spouse relationship issues, my goal is to help them learn how to have a positive attachment. In order to attach to someone, you have to be open to letting them in, letting them see who you really are, being willing to give, willing to ask them to give, appreciating what is good about them, and thinking and saying positive words about them.

How do you show love to your children? What could you be doing more to show you love them? What is their "love language"? Even if your child is very different from you, do you point out their

---

[135] Quoted by Foster Cline

160

strengths and meet them where they are? Do you hug them often, look for opportunities to hold their hand, scratch their back, or twirl them around? Do you spend time with them and find ways to have fun together? Do you apologize when you have hurt them? We all have ways we could love better. Take a moment to reflect on how you could show your children love today.

Educating Kids on Nutrition

There was very limited information about nutrition and health when I was a child, and some of it contradictory. My parents loved me very much and provided what was considered to be a well-balanced meal and healthy diet at that time. Now we have some research based, solid knowledge about macronutrients and how they affect your body, and that the standard American diet is actually a far cry from well balanced and healthy. Unfortunately, my weak body was a victim of that.

We are accountable to pass that knowledge on to our children. When the Word of Wisdom was revealed to Joseph Smith, LDS parents started to teach their children not to drink wine, tea, coffee, and to stop using tobacco.[136] The Lord has blessed us with knowledge about how over-consuming sugar is negatively affecting our cells by causing inflammation, free radicals, compromised stomach acid, addiction, mood instability, and overtaxing our liver, pancreas, heart, and kidneys. Let us share that knowledge with the next generation.

Teach Children Not to Judge

Caution your children about not judging others who may eat excessive amounts of unhealthful food. Just as children might point and whisper at the person smoking a cigarette, they may point the finger of scorn at others who eat what they have just been taught to avoid. It is natural development while kids are learning what is good

---

[136] Doctrine and Covenants, section 89

for them to distinguish what is not good, and it can spark feelings of superiority, judgment, fear, jealousy, or even disgust. Children think in more concrete terms than adults so they are more susceptible to judge themselves or others harshly when something is "bad," even to the point of thinking people are bad or scary for behaving those ways. Help them remember that everyone is different, everyone is doing their best with the knowledge they have, and it is not our place to judge.

This may be helped if you explain clearly why you are getting rid of the cookies, carefully educating children that certain food is medicine for brain and optimal gut health. Include that our bodies have mechanisms to deal with food that is not helpful, so they don't need to be afraid of food, we just need to do what we can to nourish ourselves. Be clear about what is really unwise and what is fine without demonizing food or people.

Books on Nutrition for Kids

On my website, you can find a book called *Sugar and Your Body* designed for younger readers. I wrote this book to help parents explain to their children specifically why there is a need for being careful about over-eating sugar. Read and discuss what they felt was true about it after. Research other good books that have nutritional information for children or teens.

Eating Wisely vs. Eating Disorder

When educating children be as careful as you possibly can not to create paranoia and obsession in your children. Eating disorders primarily stem from messages in the environment that how a person looks is not good enough. But even paranoia that certain foods are "bad" can become an obsession and a phobia. Pray for guidance to find balance in educating them.

If you have a child who is refusing to eat, seems self-conscious about her looks, and/or is dropping weight, you need to intervene. However, backing off attempts to feed kids healthy meals and encouraging your child to eat sugar and candy is not the correct intervention. I can understand a mother's concern completely; however, it is still true that too much sugar is not good for your child whether she is skinny, fat, or otherwise, and eating whole, nutrient dense foods with lots of vitamins and minerals is good for her. Of course we don't want a child to have an eating disorder, but encouraging her or him to eat food that will deplete the body instead of nourish it, and cause a myriad of long term problems, is not the answer.

In some cases, you may have to intervene by taking your child to a psychologist who can find where the underlying emotions are that are creating the problem. In most cases, the parents can process the child's concerns with them at home. Education, collaboration, empathy, and working together with our kids to find their unique metabolic type may be an answer.

Notice, Empathize and Brainstorm

Ross Greene illustrates a wonderful way to preemptively talk to your child about your concerns without imposing your will or opinion.[137] Let them put their concerns on the table, validate that, then put your concerns on the table, and allow them to come up with a solution to all the concerns. If your child is self-conscious about his or her size and stops eating, he/she may also be reticent to share his/her concerns about it, fearing you will not understand and will give a lecture. There may be a chance your child really wants to talk, but will test you to see if you really want to let them in. Make sure you don't push it.

Here is an illustration of observing, inquiring, and collaborating with a child:

"Anne I notice you didn't eat the cookie your teacher gave you today. What's up?"

"I just didn't want it."

---

[137] Ross W. Greene, PhD. *The Explosive Child*

"Oh you didn't want it. Sometimes I choose not to eat cookies too. I noticed you didn't eat much at dinner either. What's up?"

"I wasn't that hungry."

"I see, you weren't hungry. Is there any other reason you weren't hungry?"

"No."

"Well, if you ever want to talk about it, I'm here to listen."

(The next day after dinner.)

"Anne, how are you feeling?"

"Tired."

"That's hard. I feel tired sometimes too."

"I'm a little hungry too."

"Would you like some leftovers? I noticed you didn't eat much again and figured you were just not hungry."

"I'm hungry. I just don't want to get too fat."

"You are worried about getting fat. What's up?"

"Well, Chris and Tyler are really skinny, and I'm not, so I thought maybe I eat too much."

"That sounds hard."

"Yeah, but it's also because Kate told me I had a big belly and arms, and I was embarrassed."

"That would make me feel embarrassed too. So you are concerned that if you eat as much as you want, you will get fat, and you want to be skinny like Chris and Tyler?"

"Yeah, it's not fair they get to eat."

"I understand your concern. It's just that I am concerned that if you don't eat, your body will go into starvation mode, and you will get sick when you eat and your blood sugar will be low. That makes you feel really tired."

"Do you think that's why I'm tired?"

"Maybe. What do you think we could do to help your body get the food it needs without making you fat?"

"I don't know."

"Well, I have some ideas but I think you could figure out what is best for your body."

"Maybe I could eat more dinner and never have dessert."

"That's an idea. We could try that for a while. Can I do anything to help with that?"

"Maybe you could not have desserts around the house, then I won't feel bad that everyone gets them but me."

"Ok I can do that."

Notice that the parent did not try to convince their child they were beautiful, or not fat at all, didn't tell them they were wrong, didn't try to correct their solution, or dismiss their ideas and concerns. The parent simply listened and validated, so the child felt heard and understood, and then allowed them to come up with a solution.

If the solution doesn't work, it's OK. You can have another conversation with them about what you noticed, i.e. "I notice you felt really angry when you couldn't have cake at the party..." Observe, inquire, empathize and let your child come up with some solutions so you and your child can collaboratively find a balance between caring too much and not caring at all.

Spiritual Principle 8: Teaching Children to Look to God

We desire to help our children choose the right, which involves teaching them correct principles and letting them govern themselves. Children can't know the dangers of gluttony if we don't teach them. King Benjamin advised us to "teach them to walk in the ways of truth and soberness."[138] I echo his charge.

I, like Nephi, desire to write the words of truth and "send them forth unto all my children." I pray often that the words of eternal life and the Spirit will be what fills my children's souls. "Wherefore, do not spend money for that which is of no worth, nor your labor for that which cannot satisfy. Hearken diligently unto me, and remember the words which I have spoken; and come unto the Holy One of

---

[138] The Book of Mormon, Mosiah 4:15

Israel, and feast upon that which perisheth not, neither can be corrupted, and let your soul delight in fatness."[139]

Next time you are tempted to give a treat to your kids to reinforce a behavior, consider sharing God's love with them instead. It is free to all and you can "eat and share" as much of it as you want. Fill their hearts with words of affirmation, reminders of their potential, gratitude for our Savior so they don't have empty voids they want to fill with food. Sing to them, praise the Lord, dance, play, work together, pray together. This will teach them that when they are adults, instead of focusing on the next temporal fix, they can look to God to ease their suffering.

The Lord beckons and reassures us, "Come, my brethren, every one that thirsteth, come ye to the waters; and he that hath no money, come buy and eat; yea come buy wine and milk without money and without price."[140]

Challenge 8: Challenges for Kids

There are many challenges you could come up with for your kids. My favorite is the gallon Ziplock challenge. This is a great way to give a visual to your children of how much corrupt food they are consuming. For this challenge, children decide to go dessert and candy free for one month, and freeze every candy and dessert they would have eaten but declined in a gallon Ziplock. After the month, they can see how much refined sugar their bodies would have had to process. You can see how much toil you are sparing your body.

The behavioral contract for kids is often a good way to help them stay strong in eating wisely. Just as it does for adults, the behavioral contract helps children develop self-control and coping skills by committing them to a time-limited goal. Remember to use rewards that are not edible to help them get away from the idea that excessive sweets are an appropriate reinforcement.

---

[139] The Book of Mormon, 2 Nephi 9:51
[140] The Book of Mormon, 2 Nephi 9:50

Other ideas might include letting your kids make their own personal diet lifestyle and eating goals, using the template in chapter six, and doing it with them. Challenge them to eat whole for one meal every day. Teach them how to cook and give them opportunities to cook for you. You might offer to pay them to come up with a healthy dinner idea each night so they will be willing to eat it. Read "Sugar and Your Body" together, or other books at their level to help them understand the importance of nutrition.

Just pick one challenge and try it. Their direction towards health begins as soon as you can help them on that path, and it's never too late to start.

Epilogue

Precious are the years to come, while the righteous gather home for the great millennium, when they'll rest in blessedness. Prudent in this world of woes, they will triumph o'er their foes while the realm of Zion grows purer for eternity.

LDS Hymn 25[141]

Recap

The whole program may be summed up in the following guide, which came to my mind one day while attending the temple. It's a fun and easy way to remember the principles.

Wellness Begins with W

Wonder: what does my body need to eat today?

Whole: find a recipe and modify it with whole foods

Work: prepare your meal yourself with love, no shortcuts

Wait: Thank the Lord and bless your food

Wisdom: slow down to eat, be mindful of how you feel

Wash: clean up after your meal

What you gain: Wise mind and healthy body

As a recap, I've outlined the program steps, the spiritual principles, and challenges at the end of each step. Now that you have read and undertaken these challenges, how has your life changed? I hope it has given you a powerful paradigm shift.

---

[141] "Now We'll Sing With One Accord" verse 4

Program Step	Spiritual Principle	Challenge
Food Awareness	Learning and Prayer	Research food corruptions
Observe Inside Forces	Discipline and Sacrifice	Write down thoughts related to food
Observe Outside Forces	Faith	Fill out a food diary
Dare to Change	Fasting	7 day, 1 meal whole food challenge
Loving Food and Life	Acceptance/Gratitude	10 day whole food challenge
Optimal Diet Lifestyle	Repentance	Discover your Optimal Diet Lifestyle
Vitality a choice	Patience/Obedience	Implement optimal diet
Educating Children	Teaching Children to Look to God	Challenges for kids

Fight for the Right

As mentioned, when I started writing this book I first came up with the acronym FOODFIGHT with nine steps. As I wrote the book I decided it was better to take the word "fight" out of the equation, because I wanted to emphasize that acceptance, gratitude, and love were much more powerful approaches to take to achieve true change. However, there is a measure of fighting that has to happen, and that is not a bad thing. Fighting for something we believe in shows love.

When Captain Moroni urged his people to stand up and fight for their freedom, he hoisted the title of liberty, which reminded them their love for their families, their country, and their freedom.[142] Sometimes we have to fight for something we love. Every day we wake up and put on the armor of God, preparing ourselves for another day of battling the adversary and standing for truth, for the love of ourselves, our families, our freedom, and our God.

---

[142] The Book of Mormon, Alma 46

We are here to learn how to trust God even though our minds are veiled, to have joy, and to prepare to meet God. Everything around us is dust! Material things mean nothing in the eternal perspective. We are being tested to see if we can look past the money, food, clothes, upsets, housing, and treasure things of eternity. We only live for a brief moment. Trust God and stay true to Him no matter how difficult and confusing things become.

We want to be able to say "I fought a good fight!" Don't give up. Hold the vision and trust the process. Love your life and love your food enough to fight for your life by guarding against food corruptions.

Power of Spiritual Principles

There may be other ways people can improve their diet and their health than what I've come up with, but I like this program because it fosters spiritual growth at the same time. Whether you are learning how to overcome a sugar addiction or building schools in third world countries, doing something difficult will only benefit your soul if coupled with spiritual principles. The *Wise Food Mind* program will improve your health, but the overarching goal is to improve your spirit.

Prayer lets God know we need Him, seek His direction, trust Him, and are grateful for what we have been blessed with. Discipline and sacrifice put our wills on the altar, showing we are willing to do God's will. Faith goes in the direction God has given you without knowing how you will get there or even where you may be going.

Fasting is a specific form of sacrifice that trains your body to control bodily appetites for a greater cause and purges you of selfishness. Acceptance and gratitude give you peace as you do something difficult and face pain.

Repentance is a new understanding of a better way to live, and whether we understand why or not, turns us to God and shows we trust Him. Patience and obedience give us the ability to endure to the end with trust. Teaching children correct principles shows we have enough trust to give those we love most in the world the same instruction.

Living Life Joyfully

The week I wrote this epilogue Elder Richard G. Scott passed away. I felt a pang of sadness and wanted to cry, and realized that was the first time I'd felt healthy mourning at the passing of another person. In the past, I'd felt envious of those who pass away or relieved they weren't suffering anymore. That shows how miserable I was! This time was different because I had improved my quality of life to the point that I have more joy than suffering, even though life is still hard at times. How grateful I am to not feel overwhelmed about how to endure another day, but rather feel joy to be alive.

Life is not perfect. I still have days when I am tired, moments when my head throbs, times when I am hurt by something someone said or did. But rather than letting those times cause me to murmur and complain, I can lift my voice and make a joyful noise unto the Lord, knowing that in this life we will have tribulation, but Heavenly Father has promised us the gift of salvation after we have done all we can do. My desire now is to sing songs of thanks, like the "Thanksgiving Hosanna" my mom wrote, which states,

> Let us shout hosanna to thee for enabling us to be free,
> With the choice to follow thee with a perfect hope for thy face to see.
> What a glorious day it will be when in grand thanksgiving to thee
> We will join the choirs above singing ceaseless praises of love
> To thy honor and glory and power and might!
> Rejoicing to be in the light of thy love for eternity.[143]

---

[143] Lyrics from "Thanksgiving Hosanna" composed and written by Kathy Sue Barrett

Becoming a Zion People

I imagine my joy could be even greater if others achieved this thankful heart and peace as well. The scriptures define "Zion" as "the pure in heart."[144] The result of incorporating the above spiritual principles is achieving humility, refinement, and becoming more like our Father in Heaven. I hope that you not only fight food corruptions and reclaim health, but become closer to God and stronger in these God-like qualities.

> Verily I say, that inasmuch as ye do this, the fullness of the earth is yours...
>
> Yea the herb, and the good things which come of the earth, whether for food or raiment, or for houses or for barns, or for orchards, or for gardens, or for vineyards;
>
> Yea, all things which come of the earth, in the season thereof, are made for the benefit and use of man, both to please the eye and to gladden the heart;
>
> Yea, ...to strengthen the body and to enliven the soul.
>
> And it pleaseth God that he hath given all these things unto man; for unto this end were they made to be used, with judgment, not to excess, neither by extortion.
>
> D&C 59: 16-20

I testify this will be true for you, as it has been for me. You have taken a courageous and disciplined step towards a life-time of ultimate self-reliance, purification of your mind and body, and control over your appetites. Qualities of a Zion people.

---

[144] Bible dictionary under "Zion"

About the Author

Heather Barrett Schauers is from Lindon, Utah, mother of four beautiful souls, three of which are living, and married to her eternal companion Jared. She earned her Masters of Social Work degree from BYU and currently works as a therapist at Successful Therapy. Heather has a passion for helping people with mental health issues, addictions, and healing through nutrition. She spends her time writing, reading, nurturing, cooking, teaching, and praising the Lord for the gift of salvation.

For more information about Heather or to contact her, visit www.wisefoodmind.com or her blog wisefoodmind.blogspot.com

Resources

Airola, P. *Hypoglycemia: A Better Approach.* Oregon: Health Plus Pub., 1977.

Axe, J. "Food is Medicine." Lecture from Psychology of Eating *Future of Healing* conference (2015).

Bowden, J. "A Renegade Look at Nutrition." Lecture from Psychology of Eating *Future of Healing* conference (2015).

Brogan, K. "Women, Food and Health."Lecture from Psychology of Eating *Future of Healing* conference (2015).

Burns, D. D. *The Feeling Good Handbook.* Plume, 1999.

Burns, D. D. *When Panic Attacks: the new drug free anxiety therapy that can change your life.* New York: Harmony, 2007.

Cook, W. *Foodwise: Understanding What We Eat and How it Affects Us, The Story of Human Nutrition.* Clairview Books, 2003.

David, M. *Nourishing Wisdom.* New York: Bell tower, 1991.

DesMaisons, K. *The Sugar Addicts Total Recovery Program.* New York: Ballantine, 2000.

Dufty, W. *Sugar Blues.* Grand Central Life and Style, 1986.

Elkaim, Y. "Nutrition Engergy and Fatigue." Lecture from Psychology of Eating *Future of Healing* conference (2015).

Fed Up Documentary, with Katie Couric. Directed by Stephanie Soechtig. Anchor Bay Studios, 2014.

Gabriel, J. "The Gabriel Method Approach to Weight." Lecture from Psychology of Eating *Future of Healing* conference (2015).

Geanopulos, S. "Your Diagnosis: Why labels can be dangerous and prevent you from seeing what else is happening." Lecture from The Center for Epigenetic Expression *The Pain Relief Project*, 2015.

Gershon, M.D. *The Second Brain: A Groundbreaking New Understanding of Nervous Disorders of the Stomach and Intestine.* Harper Perennial, 1999.

Gotschall, E. *Breaking the Vicious Cycle: Intestinal Health Through Diet.* Kirkton Press, 1994.

Greene, R.W. *The Explosive Child.* Harper Paperbacks, 2001.

Gunnarson, G. "Nourishment, Health and Presence." Lecture from Psychology of Eating *Future of Healing* conference (2015).

Hyman, M. "The Future of Nutrition." Lecture from Psychology of Eating *Future of Healing* conference (2015).

Hymn Book of The Church of Jesus Christ of Latter-day Saints.

Kaufman, F. *Diabesity: A Doctor and Her Patients on the Front Lines of the Obesity-Diabetes Epidemic.* Bantam, 2006.

Kent, C. "Stress: Good and Bad." Lecture from The Center for Epigenetic Expression *The Pain Relief Project*, 2015.

Kharrazian, D. "The Gut-Brain Axis: How to Train Your Brain for Better Bowl Movements." Lecture from Underground Wellness *Digestion Sessions* with Sean Croxton (2014).

Korn, L. "Nutritional and Complementary Treatments for Mental Health Disorders." Lecture recorded by PESI Publishing and Media, Jan 2014.

Logan, A. *The Brain Diet: The Connection Between Nutrition Mental Health, and Intelligence*, p. 1-20. New York: Cumberland House Publishing, 2007.

Lounsbury, H. *Fix Your Mood with Food: The "Live Natural, Live Well" Approach To Whole Body Health.* Skirt!, 2014.

Lustig, R. *Fat Chance: Beating the Odds Against Sugar, Processed Food, Obesity, and Disease.* Plume, 2012.

Lustig, R. "The Bitter Truth." Lecture from The University of California, 2009.

Mowll, B. "A New Look at Diabetes." Lecture from Psychology of Eating *Future of Healing* conference (2015).

National Eating Disorders Website: nationaleatingdisorders.org/orthorexia

Nelson, B. *The Emotion code: How to Release Your Trapped Emotions for Abundant Health, Love and Happiness.* Wellness Unmasked Publishing, 2007.

O'Malley, M. *The Gift of Our Compulsions.* Digital print, 2004.

O'Bryan, T. "Extinguishing Inflammation: Putting Out the Fire with Real Foods." Lecture from Underground Wellness *Digestion Sessions* with Sean Croxton (2014).

O'Malley, M. "What's in the Way IS the Way." Lecture from Psychology of Eating *Future of Healing* conference (2015).

Orechhio, C. "Healing the Digestive System." Lecture from Psychology of Eating *Future of Healing* conference (2015).

Orechhio, C. "How to Kick Candida for Good." Lecture from Underground Wellness *Digestion Sessions* with Sean Croxton (2014).

Perlmutter, D. "Brain Health, Food, and the Gut." Lecture from Psychology of Eating *Future of Healing* conference (2015).

Perlmutter, D. *Grain Brain: The Surprising Truth about Wheat, Carbs, and Sugar--Your Brain's Silent Killers.* Little, Brown and Co., 2013.

Pershing, A. "Important Insights into Overeating and Dieting." Lecture from Psychology of Eating *Future of Healing* conference (2015).

Pleasure Unwoven: An Explanation of the Brain Disease of Addiction. Documentary with Kevin McCauley. Institute for Addiction Study Studios, 2009.

Poulson, M. *Brain Diet: Brain Nutrition for Instant Brain Boost and Healthy Brain Function at Any Age.* Amazon Digital Services, 2014.

Pritcher, A. *Health Bent: 50 Everyday Nutrition, Exercise, Medical, Mental, & Lifestyle Habits to Improve Your Health,* p. 1-3. Amazon Digital Services, 2015.

Rosen, E. "Eating Psychology and Mind Body Nutrition." Lecture from Psychology of Eating *Future of Healing* conference (2015).

Ruscio, M. "Solving Diarrhea" Lecture from Underground Wellness *Digestion Sessions* with Sean Croxton (2014).

Sanfilippo, D. *The 21 Day Sugar Detox.* Victory Belt Publishing, 2013.

Somov, P. G. "360 Degrees of Mindful Eating: Five Core Skill Sets to Overcome Overeating." Seminar by Premier Education Solutions, 2009.

Soszka, S. "The Gut Mood Connection: How digestive problems cause depression and anxiety." Lecture from Underground Wellness *Digestion Sessions* with Sean Croxton (2014).

"Statistics About Diabetes." *American Diabetes Association*. N.p., n.d. Web. 2015.

The Book of Mormon. The Church of Jesus Christ of Latter-day Saints.

The Holy Bible, King James Version.

Virgin, J.J. "The Sugar Impact Diet." Lecture from Psychology of Eating *Future of Healing* conference (2015).

Walsh, W. J. *Nutrient Power: Heal your biochemistry and heal your brain*. Skyhorse, 2014.

Wright, S. "The Specific Carbohydrate Diet and Digestive Health." Lecture from Psychology of Eating *Future of Healing* conference (2015).

Young, R. and Young, S. *The pH Miracle*. Grand Central Life and Style, 2010.

Heading Index

Made in the USA
Charleston, SC
29 March 2016